## Welcome to
# LEGENDARY GUITARS

**HISTORIC INSTRUMENTS & AMPS FROM THE GOLDEN ERA**

Vintage guitars are, by definition, of the past – relics that hark back to a bygone era. But unlike so many celebrated inventions of the mid-20th century, the iconic instruments that appear on these pages have not been rendered culturally or technologically irrelevant. Quite the opposite, in fact. You only need glance at the extensive retro-themed offerings from Fender, Gibson, Epiphone, Gretsch, Rickenbacker and Martin to realise axes like these have never been more essential. In today's all-too-often transient world, these timeless designs are a grounding, hands-on connection with the past and the present. The passage of time has only served to broaden and deepen the universal appeal of such guitars, as the family tree of rock 'n' roll has grown and spread its roots far and wide. If ever there was something positive to be gleaned from the modern era – something that brings real joy and meaning to millions – it is our music. Championing outcasts and underdogs while hailing beauty and virtuosity, here are just some of the legendary guitars that made it possible...

# LEGENDARY GUITARS

## HISTORIC INSTRUMENTS & AMPS FROM THE GOLDEN ERA

**Future Publishing Ltd**
Quay House
The Ambury
Bath BA1 1UA
+44 (0) 1225 442244

### Editorial
Editor-in-Chief **Jamie Dickson**
Art Editor **Darren Phillips**
Editor & Writer **Rod Brakes**
Managing Editor **Lucy Rice**
Editorial Director, Bookazines **Jon White**
Head of Design, Bookazines, Knowledge **Greg Whitaker**
Senior Art Editor, Bookazines **Andy Downes**

### Advertising
Media packs are available on request
Commercial Director **Clare Dove**
clare.dove@futurenet.com

### International
Head of Print Licensing **Rachel Shaw**
licensing@futurenet.com

### Circulation
Head of Commerical Development **Tim Mathers**

### Production
Group Head of Production **Mark Constance**
Senior Production Manager **Matt Eglinton**
Production Managers **Nola Cokely,**
**Vivienne Calvert, Frances Twentyman**
Production Analyst **Keely Miller**
Senior Advertising Production Manager **Jo Crosby**
Digital Editions Manager **Jason Hudson**

### Management
SVP Consumer **Kevin Addley**
Managing Director, Music, Photography & Design **Stuart Williams**
Content Director, Music **Scott Rowley**

### Printed by
William Gibbons, 26 Planetary Road, Willenhall,
West Midlands, WV13 3XT

### Distributed by
Marketforce UK, 121-141 Westbourne Terrace, London W2 6QA
mfcommunications@futurenet.com www.marketforce.co.uk

### Disclaimer
All contents © 2024 Future Publishing Limited or published under licence. All rights reserved. No part of this magazine may be used, stored, transmitted or reproduced in any way without the prior written permission of the publisher. Future Publishing Limited (company number 2008885) is registered in England and Wales. Registered office: Quay House, The Ambury, Bath BA1 1UA. All information contained in this publication is for information only and is, as far as we are aware, correct at the time of going to press. Future cannot accept any responsibility for errors or inaccuracies in such information. You are advised to contact manufacturers and retailers directly with regard to the price of products/services referred to in this publication. Apps and websites mentioned in this publication are not under our control. We are not responsible for their contents or any other changes or updates to them. This magazine is fully independent and not affiliated in any way with the companies mentioned herein.

**Legendary Guitars Edition Two**
© 2024 Future Publishing Limited

---

**FUTURE** Connectors. Creators. Experience Makers.

Future plc is a public company quoted on the London Stock Exchange (symbol: FUTR)
www.futureplc.com

Chief Executive Officer **Jon Steinberg**
Non-Executive Chairman **Richard Huntingford**
Chief Financial and Strategy Officer **Penny Ladkin-Brand**

Tel +44 (0)1225 442 244

ipso. For press freedom with responsibility

Recycle — We are committed to only using magazine paper which is derived from responsibly managed, certified forestry and chlorine-free manufacture. The paper in this bookazine was sourced and produced from sustainable managed forests, conforming to strict environmental and socioeconomic standards.

Part of the

# Guitarist
bookazine series

# INTRODUCING
# FABLE
## GRANULAR SOUNDSCAPE GENERATOR

Let your storybook adventure grow with the Fable Granular Soundscape Generator. The Fable gives you five all-new programs centered around sample and chop delay algorithms to create bizarrely beautiful networks of sampled and resampled sounds. To create it's glitchy environment, the Fable uses two DSP chips running in series, each with their own analog feedback path, to create rich themes of reversing, time-stretching, pitch-shifting, and vast ambiance.

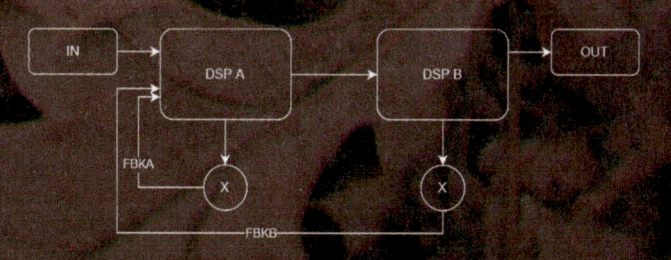

**Explore more at walrusaudio.com**

FACE  Exclusive UK-Distribution - www.face.be

# Contents

**ELECTRIC GUITARS**
## 08

**GUITAR AMPLIFIERS**
## 90

# Contents

## LEGENDARY GUITARS

ACOUSTIC GUITARS 108

### ELECTRIC GUITARS
10 ..........Rickenbacker Guitars
20 ..........Rickenbacker 12-String Capris
22 ..........Fender Telecaster
28 ..........Fender Telecaster Custom
30 ..........CBS Fender Telecasters
32 ..........1950s Fender Stratocasters
34 ..........1960s Fender Stratocasters
36 ..........Fender Jazzmaster
38 ..........Fender Jaguar
40 ..........Fender Electric XII
42 ..........Fender VI
44 ..........Gibson & Fender Bass Guitars
52 ..........Gibson Electric Archtops
54 ..........Gibson ES-175
56 ..........Gibson ES-125TDC
58 ..........Gibson ES-330TD
60 ..........Gibson ES-335TD
62 ..........Gibson Les Paul Standard
64 ..........Late-60s Gibson Les Paul Custom
66 ..........Gibson Les Paul/SG Standard
68 ..........Gibson Melody Makers
70 ..........Reverse Gibson Firebirds
72 ..........Non-Reverse Gibson Firebirds
74 ..........Epiphone History
80 ..........Epiphone Casino E230TD
82 ..........Epiphone Riviera E360TD
84 ..........Gretsch Chet Atkins Signatures
86 ..........Gretsch 6128 Duo Jet
88 ..........Gretsch White Falcon

### AMPLIFIERS
92 ..........Fender Tweed Amps
94 ..........Fender 'Tweed' Bassman
96 ..........Fender Reverb
98 ..........Fender Princeton Reverb
100 ..........Vox AC30 Twin
102 ..........Marshall JTM 45 MK II
104 ..........Marshall Amps
106 ..........Orange Amps

### ACOUSTIC GUITARS
110 ..........19th & 20th Century Martins
116 ..........Martin D-18
118 ..........Martin 0-18
120 ..........Gibson 'Dreadnought' Jumbos
122 ..........Gibson J-45
124 ..........Gibson SJ-200
126 ..........Gibson LG Series
128 ..........Epiphone F.T. 110/Frontier

LEGENDARY GUITARS | 7

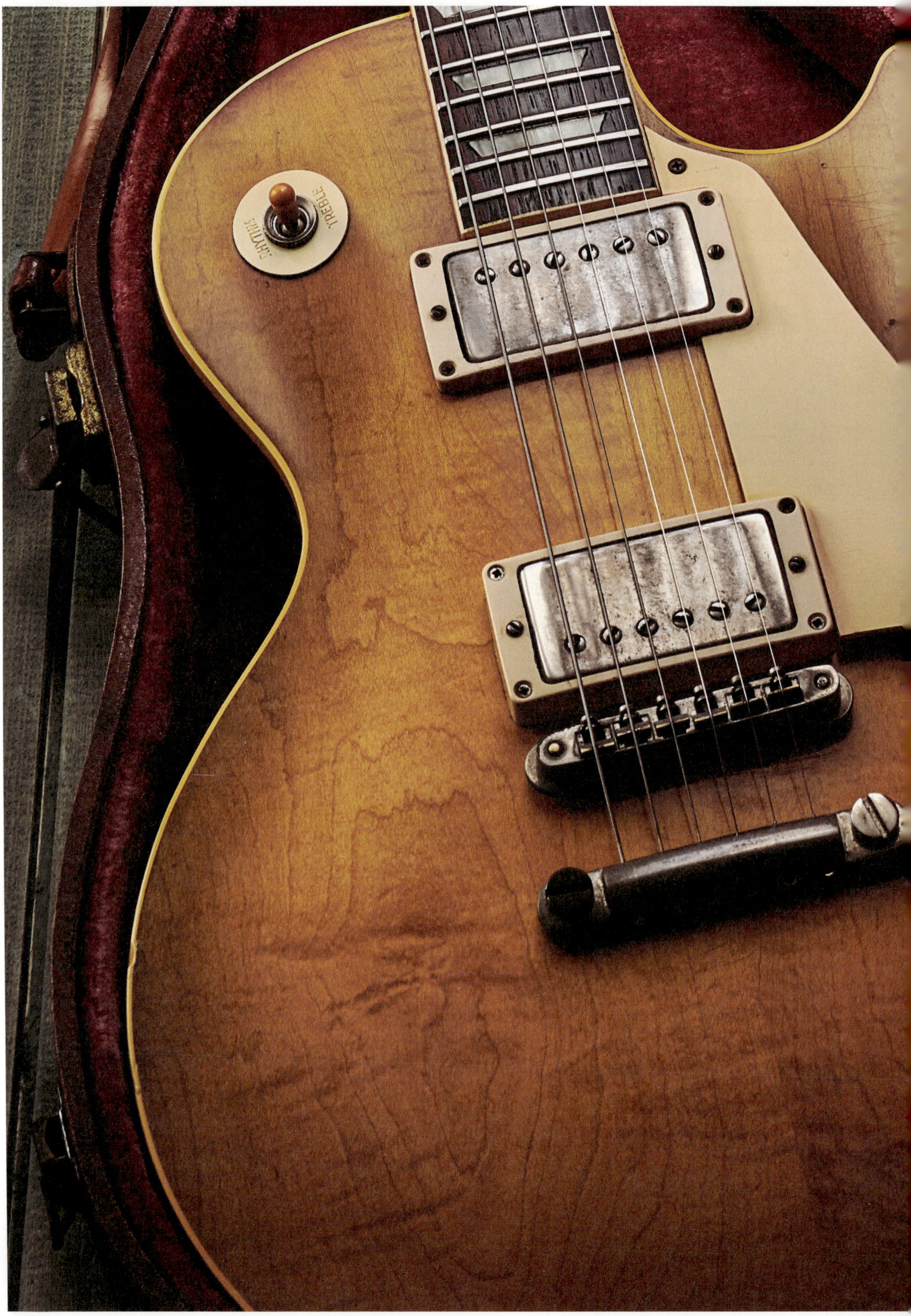
RHYTHM
TREBLE

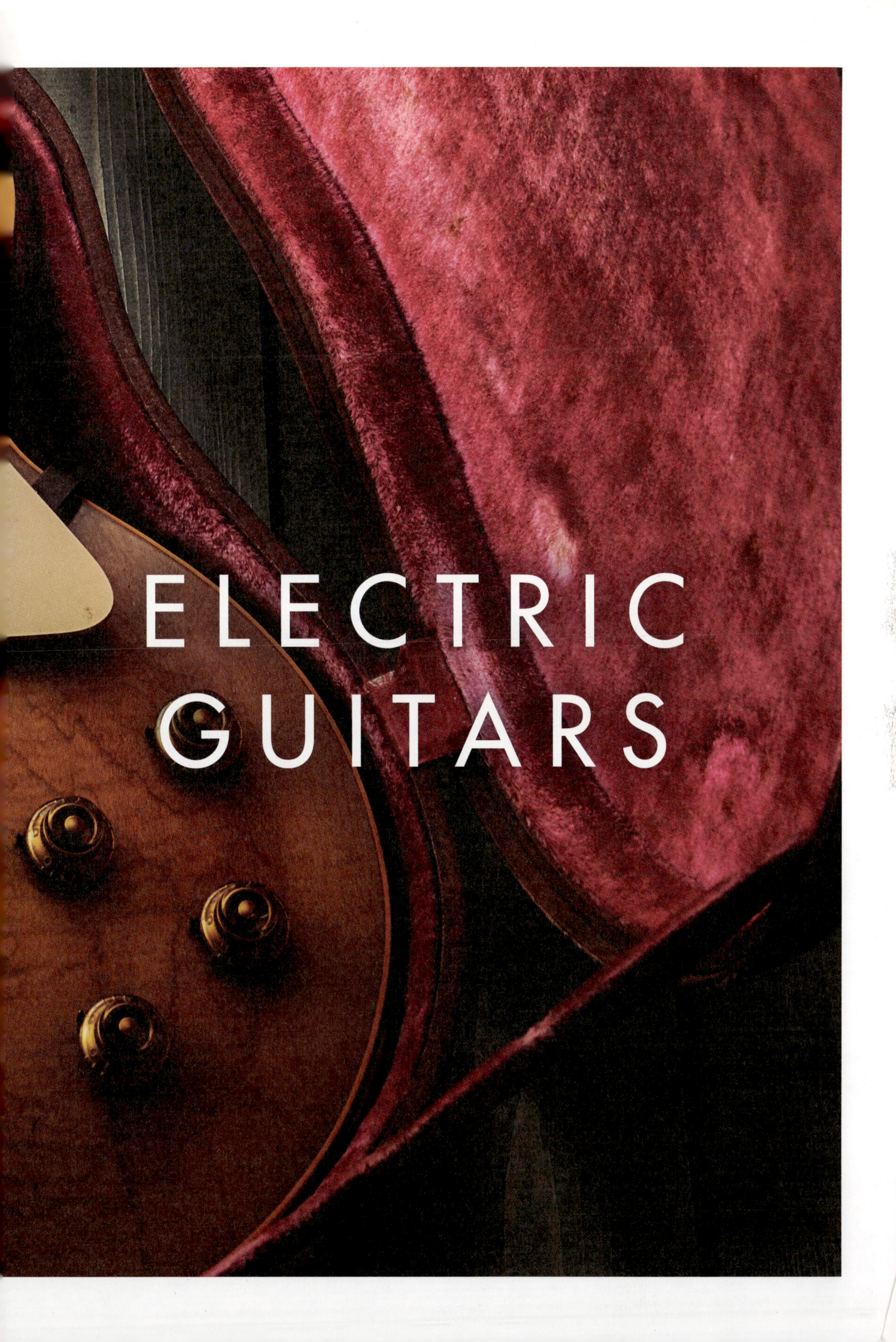

# ELECTRIC GUITARS

# Rick 'N' Roll

Martin Kelly, co-author of *Fender: The Golden Age 1946-1970* and *Rickenbacker Guitars 1931-1999: Out Of The Frying Pan Into The Fireglo*, retraces the evolution of Rickenbacker guitars

**Words** Rod Brakes  **Photography** Olly Curtis

Around 90 years ago, guitarist George Beauchamp (pronounced 'BEE-chum') invented the world's first commercially viable electric guitar, which – along with its 'horseshoe' pickup – sparked a revolution in guitar design and sounds. With his fellow National String Instrument Corporation associates Paul Barth and Adolph Rickenbacher, George promptly formed the Ro-Pat-In company in order to take his new invention to market with a focus on electric Spanish guitars and lap steels. It soon became known as the Electro String Instrument Corporation, and the firm eventually settled on the more familiar Rickenbacker name (an anglicised version of Adolph Rickenbacher's Swiss surname). Since then, Rickenbacker has remained one of the most important brands in pop culture and, to this day, continues to build some of the world's finest electric guitars at its California base.

"A lot of people think Rickenbacker started out with lap steels only, but they actually brought both electric Spanish and lap steels out at the same time,"

Rickenbacker Guitars | FEATURE

FEATURE | **Rickenbacker Guitars**

**01**

> *"Electric record players had two pickup coils either side of the needle, and George Beauchamp used this principle as the basis for the first electric guitar pickup"*

**01**
Rickenbackers are more versatile than they are often given credit for, but they undeniably excel in the melodic pop role, as Peter Buck of REM so powerfully demonstrated

begins Martin Kelly. "I think there's a bit of a misunderstanding that the lap steel was where they began. In truth, they knew that the application for electric Spanish guitars was there from the outset."

While writing Rickenbacker's definitive history, *Rickenbacker Guitars 1931-1999: Out Of The Frying Pan Into The Fireglo*, Martin's painstaking research has taken him across the globe in search of answers. Today, however, we are the ones in need of answers as we stand agog at the incredible collection of vintage Rickys that Martin and his brother, photographer and filmmaker Paul Kelly, have kindly brought along to the *Guitarist* studios to share with us all.

So, how did the idea for the horseshoe pickup originally come about?

"To cut a long story short, George was desperate to make guitars louder," Martin tells us. "In the 1920s, him and John Dopyera came up with the resonator guitar. You know how really old record players use a needle, a diaphragm and a horn? Well, George thought about putting a diaphragm under the bridge and that's how him and John Dopyera came up with the [National] resonator design. Later, he turned to the record player principle again, but this time it was electric. He realised that electric record players had two pickup coils either side of the needle and used this principle, replacing the needle with a guitar string. That was

the basis for the first electric guitar pickup, and he used horseshoe-shaped magnets to strengthen the signal.

"The pickup on this [1933 Electro Spanish, right] has six flush polepieces, but they aren't magnetised; they're just ferrous metal slugs. A couple of years later, George magnetised the polepieces, which increased the power of the pickup. Bodies and necks were outsourced. This Electro Spanish has a Harmony body onto which they simply mounted the pickup enabling the guitarist to be heard. George did some other pickup designs, including one where the magnets face in a different direction. He genuinely is the father of the electric guitar!"

While George Beauchamp was trying to get a patent issued for the pickup, its radical design was being ruthlessly copied by several other manufacturers.

"Rival makers quickly adopted George's design with pickups that were more or less exact copies." says Martin. "For a while, people must have presumed Rickenbacker were supplying Vega and other brands with pickups, but they weren't. Competitors simply thought, 'That's a good idea – we should make these, too.' And because the patent hadn't cleared, no-one could stop them. This went on for years, and there were two main reasons why the patent application wouldn't clear. Firstly, the patent office couldn't decide if it was a musical

PHOTO BY EBET ROBERTS/REDFERNS/GETTY IMAGES

12 | LEGENDARY GUITARS

# 1933 ELECTRO SPANISH
# 1935 ELECTRO TENOR GUITAR

"This [1933 Electro Spanish, pictured right] has a conventional 14-fret neck join and the top is made from thick plywood," says Martin. "I think that would have been specially requested so it could carry the pickup, which weighs a ton. The slotted headstock has the early 'wing' Rickenbacker logo. Rick worked out early on that the volume control was useful. The [1935] Electro Tenor Guitar is a 'B-series' (Bakelite) instrument, and the frets are moulded in. These came out in 1934 and they also made a regular six-string version. It's small, but you'd hold it like a regular guitar. In a way, this is the first solidbody guitar."

FEATURE | **Rickenbacker Guitars**

*"The 'toaster' pickup came in during '57 and ushered in that defining Rickenbacker chime. It looks like a humbucker, but it's actually a single coil"*

**02**
Paul Weller, pictured here with The Jam, was one of a new wave of artists who took the Rickenbacker sound into the post-punk era

instrument or an electrical appliance. At the time, it was so radical there was no precedent set that these two things could actually be one and the same. It was a case of: is it an electrical appliance or a musical instrument? So it was going back and forth between departments and, in the meantime, everyone was copying the idea. The other reason was that they just didn't believe it could work. In the end, Adolph Rickenbacher sent [Hawaiian musician] Sol Ho'opi'i to the patent office to perform in person. That was enough to finally swing it."

Beauchamp's patent eventually cleared in 1937. By that stage, however, electric Spanish guitars had become widespread with major manufacturers such as Gibson getting in on the action, notably with its landmark ES-150 design.

"The Gibson ES-150 came along in 1936 and was mass produced. The first Rickenbackers came earlier and were also mass-produced, albeit on a much smaller scale," points out Martin. "But as Adolph [Rickenbacher] later stated, 'Once everyone else started making electric guitars, everyone started buying them.' So it was good – everybody was making them, and they were becoming more popular. The very first [electric Spanish] guitar Rickenbacker made had a 17-fret neck join, which was very unusual at the time. It was made in 1932 for a guy called Gage Brewer.

"At the same time, tenor guitars were being pushed in an effort to convert banjo players to the guitar. The banjo was so popular back then that the tenor was seen as a stepping stone towards the guitar. That's why the tenor became a thing for a while, but it was more of a fad, really. This 1935 Bakelite Electro Tenor Guitar [see previous page] has chromed steel covers over the hollowed chambers made to alleviate the weight, and the neck is bolt-on. Rickenbacker promised customers if the frets wore out, you could send in the old neck and get a replacement. I don't think there's any question Leo Fender would have taken that onboard as his electric Spanish guitars evolved from the lap steels he was building. It's all part of the history as these designs continue to converge."

Lap steels played a significant part in the development of the electric guitar early on and remained popular well into the 1950s.

"Lap steels were a big part of Rickenbacker's bread and butter, even when FC Hall bought the business in December 1953," explains Martin. "The [modern] Rickenbacker logo came in as soon as FC bought the company, and I think it may have been a Bob Perine design. He certainly did a series of ads for Rickenbacker during the mid-50s prior to being poached by Fender. After his important association with Fender, FC definitely wanted his own stake in the growing electric guitar market.

**Rickenbacker Guitars** | FEATURE

## 1954 COMBO 600
## 1957 COMBO 1000

"This blonde 1954 Combo 600 [pictured far right] is made from ash and features a German carve top," says Martin. "They probably copped the ash/blonde/black 'guard idea from Fender, but I do think FC Hall was trying to create something original here. To begin with, the Combos had a blonde finish, but Turquoise Blue became an option later. This black [1957 Combo 1000] has a thinner/pointier treble horn than the earlier 'tulip' guitars, which have thicker inward-curving cutaway horns. It's what you call a 'half-and-half' (because it's 'half tulip'). The next phase of development was where the bass horn followed suit into the familiar double-outward curve cutaway."

LEGENDARY GUITARS | 15

FEATURE | **Rickenbacker Guitars**

03

*"By complete fluke, the first 325 Capri ever made ended up being shipped to Germany where a young John Lennon picked it up in 1960"*

**03**
The Beatles' use of Rickenbackers for breakthrough TV appearances had seismic consequences for the company

"The first modern Rickenbacker electric guitars – the Combo 600 and Combo 800 – were introduced by FC Hall in 1954. He went to an industrial designer to come up with the shape and design, and [guitar designer/builder] Roger Rossmeisl refined it. The very first drawings – which I found in the company archive – were by someone else, but Roger definitely adapted and changed the design. Several of his traits are clearly evident in the early Combos. The original drawings had different headstock shapes, and Roger came up with this sweeping design. It's the same kind of thing you see on his earlier guitars – these fluid lines. FC inherited a ton of the old pickups from Adolph and I'm sure he thought, 'That's great – I've got loads of pickups, so I don't have to make any.' So, for years, the guitars had this inherent flaw where you couldn't palm-mute the strings as the magnets sit right in the way. But the guitar does sound good! It's bright and it has that inherent Rickenbacker chime to it already."

Emigrating from Germany to work for Gibson in the early 50s, Roger Rossmeisl spent a short time at the Kalamazoo factory in Michigan before departing for the sunnier climes of California and a job with FC Hall. He was also famed for his later Fender designs – notably the Telecaster Thinline, Coronado, and LTD models – but his influence at Rickenbacker cannot be overstated.

"You can see the first Combos have got a bit of Gibson in them with that top, but it's actually a German carve, which is Roger Rossmeisl's handiwork," says Martin. "The Combo 600 and Combo 800 look similar, but the 800 has two toggle switches that operate two pickups, which sit side by side under the horseshoe magnets. The 600 has one pickup and one toggle switch."

The next major phase in Ricky evolution began in '56 with the introduction of the Combo 400 and the 'tulip' body shape (named in reference to the guitar's petal-like outward-curving cutaways). By '58, this design had morphed into the sharper inward-curving dual-cutaway style of the Capri range, while Rossmeisl's hooked bass horn 'cresting wave' body shape debuted the same year with the 425 and 450 models.

"The real breakthrough with the tulip guitars was the neck-through-body design; it had never been done before," says Martin. "That was a completely original concept that offered improved sustain when it appeared in '56. The 'toaster' pickup came in during '57 and ushered in that defining Rickenbacker chime. It looks like a humbucker, but it's actually a single coil. I think the parallel lines are just there to make it look posh. But that's what gives it its 'toaster' nickname.

"So the tulip shape slowly evolved into the Capri – a new range introduced during '58. Roger Rossmeisl made a prototype with a

16 | LEGENDARY GUITARS

## 1966 365 OS
## 1967 365

"After the first Capri body shape, they stretched it lengthways into what they call a 'long body' Capri (they only made three guitars like that)," Martin tells us. "And then they stretched it sideways. Then, in '61, they widened the body shape again as per this '66 365 OS Capri [left]. The rounded top came in in '64, as per the '67 365 [right]. It follows a logical evolution. The [semi-hollowbodies] are hollowed from the rear and have the back 'plate' put on, just like the Telecaster Thinlines Roger Rossmeisl designed for Fender in the late 60s."

**FEATURE** | **Rickenbacker Guitars**

> "Rickenbackers have a delicate feel to them, but they're pretty tough. Especially the way they're built now"

**04**
Pete Townshend of The Who playing one of his f-hole, Rose-Morris-spec Rickenbacker electric guitars

carved top. FC loved the design and loaned it to an LA group, which led to it being named the Polynesian. Though FC was decidedly pleased with the design, he wanted a guitar that was simpler to build without a carved top. So the next Capri Roger built had a completely flat top and that guitar – the very one – ended up becoming John Lennon's. By complete fluke, the first 325 Capri ever made ended up being shipped to Germany where a young John Lennon picked it up in 1960. Which is amazing when you think about it because it's probably a major factor as to why Rickenbacker remains so popular to this day. The serial number of Lennon's first 325 is V81. 'V' is because it had a vibrato, and it's believed the carved top one was V80."

With The Fabs endorsing its guitars, the firm's fortunes were set to change forever.

"The Beatles were the spark," confirms Martin. "Suddenly, you've got all these British bands in the US like The Hollies, Herman's Hermits, The Zombies and The Animals turning up on American TV shows playing Rickenbackers, and all these kids are going, 'That's a cool guitar!' So many people I've interviewed told me, 'I didn't know it was an American guitar.' The British Invasion introduced this American brand to America, a bit like how The Stones did with the blues. Like it had to go to Britain to be made popular.

"Pete Townshend took it somewhere else. He really played the hell out of his Rose-Morris six- and 12-string models. If you get a 12-string, you can play pick-y stuff like [Roger] McGuinn, but if you hit it hard, you can really get the sound of those early Who records. Pete often played a 1993 with flat-wounds, and he hammered the fuck out of it. It's such a great sound and similar to how [Paul] Weller played Rickenbackers. Guy Picciotto from Fugazi is the same – he's very heavy-handed with it. If you think of those three guitarists – Townshend, Weller and Picciotto – they all play in a harder style. Rickenbackers have a delicate feel to them, but they're pretty tough. Especially the way they're built now.

"Rickenbackers are beautifully made. I think they've got a great aesthetic, which really sets them apart. They've got an iconic look and there aren't many brands who can boast that. Fender, Gibson, Gretsch and Rickenbacker really are the top four. In terms of what was designed in the first 20 years of the electric guitar, Rickenbacker are squarely in the pantheon. That's why Roger Rossmeisl is so important. To date, he's gone relatively unrecognised, although it seems more people have become aware of him within the last few years. In many ways, he was Rickenbacker." **G**

Visit https://phantombooks.com To order Martin & Paul Kelly's definitive history of Rickenbacker, *Rickenbacker Guitars 1931-1999: Out Of The Frying Pan Into The Fireglo*

# 1964 ROSE-MORRIS 1996
# 1964 ROSE-MORRIS 1993

"The Rose-Morris guitars are interesting because they were a by-product of The Beatles' association with the brand," says Martin. "The Beatles still loom large in the Rickenbacker story today and they were the catalyst for the Rose-Morris deal. That was the moment when it all blew all up for FC. The f-hole is the defining feature of these models and you see the same shape on the Fender Tele Thinline, which was essentially Roger Rossmeisl applying Rickenbacker production methods to a Fender. Pete Townshend put Rose-Morris models to good use, as well as smashing quite a few along the way!"

*Electric*Evolution

# Rickenbacker 12-String Capris

A favourite of The Beatles and The Byrds, these era-defining electrics still resonate

As far as 12-string electric guitars go, it's hard to beat a Rickenbacker Capri model. The Fender Electric XII is perhaps the greatest competitor in terms of playability and sound, and the Gibson EDS-1275 doubleneck also deserves an honourable mention. But with The Beatles' George Harrison and The Byrds' Roger McGuinn chiming away on Rickenbackers, while topping the charts on both sides of the Atlantic during the mid-60s, it's difficult to argue that a more era-defining 12-string exists.

Comprising six- and 12-string instruments, the '300 series' semi-hollowbody Capri line is to Rickenbacker what the Les Paul is to Gibson, or the Stratocaster is to Fender. An icon of the guitar world, this timeless design continues to define the company's identity and, along with the popular Rickenbacker bass family, is its greatest success. The Capri blueprint was originally developed by legendary guitar designer Roger Rossmeisl. German expat Rossmeisl had honed his craft in Europe building jazz guitars under the Roger brand before emigrating to America in 1953. The master luthier was briefly employed at Gibson before being recruited by Rickenbacker in '54, then by Fender in '62, where he also developed numerous models, including the Telecaster Thinline and Coronado.

Prototyped in late '57 and entering production early the following year, the inaugural Capris comprised four short-scale models (listed in '58 as the 310, 315, 320 and 325). These were swiftly followed by the full-scale standard (330, 335, 340 and 345) and deluxe (360, 365, 370 and 375) models. (The ascending model numbers correspond to spec as follows: two pickups/no vibrato; two pickups/vibrato; three pickups/no vibrato; and three pickups/vibrato.)

The vast majority of the first batch consisted of 325s à la John Lennon, and, by a freaky twist of fate, the young Beatle bought the very first Capri made (serial V81) in 1960 in Hamburg after it was shipped to its maker Rossmeisl's homeland! Lennon then brought it back to the US, displaying the guitar on national television during the band's record-breaking *The Ed Sullivan Show* appearance in February '64 when 73 million Americans tuned in to watch.

During the same trip, Rickenbacker boss FC Hall presented Harrison with a prototype Rickenbacker 360/12. The guitarist quickly put the new 12-string to good use on stage and in the studio, creating unprecedented global demand.

Harrison's 360/12 was developed in '63, based on the six-string 360 deluxe model, by renowned guitar builder Dick Burke at FC Hall's behest. It features a double-bound body with a flat/non-contoured

> George Harrison put the prototype 360/12 to use on stage and in the studio creating global demand

top and slash soundhole. It was the second 360/12 prototype (the first was given to country artist Suzi Arden) and sported Burke's intuitive tuner arrangement that allowed all 12 machineheads to be fitted on a regular size headstock. It also debuted Rickenbacker's now standard practice of placing the octave string on the treble side, thus allowing for punchier attack on the downstroke. In '64, the 360/12 was put into regular production alongside the 370/12. These rounded-top/bound-back guitars were followed by the non-contoured, unbound 330/12 in '65.

Within a few short years, the electric 12-string bubble had burst and demand dropped considerably. Nevertheless, those yearning for that classic mid-60s jangle needn't look any further than a Rickenbacker 12-string Capri.

The low-output 'toaster' single-coil pickup gave Capris that classic Rickenbacker chime and jangle. It was superseded by the Hi-gain pickup in the late 60s

## The Evolution of the 12-String Capri

### 1957
'Polynesian' semi-hollow Capri range prototype; carved top

### 1958
Capri range introduced; flat top; most short-scale with f-hole; long-scale with slash soundhole

### Summer 1963
First 360-style 12-string prototype (Arden); Fireglo finish; gold pickguard; 'cooker' knobs

### Late 1963
Second 360-style 12-string prototype (Harrison); Fireglo finish; white pickguard; black knobs

### 1964
360/12 and 370/12 introduced; rounded top; slash soundhole; bound back; triangular markers; special order 'OS' (Old Style) with non-contoured/flat top available

### Summer 1964
Rose-Morris (UK distributor) model 1993

### 1965
330/12 introduced; non-contoured top; unbound; slash soundhole; dot markers

### 1966
Jetglo (black) finish option added to Fireglo (sunburst) and Mapleglo/Natural options; 336/12 and 366/12 introduced (converter comb)

### 1967
Azureglo finish option

### 1968
Burgundyglo finish option

*Electric*Evolution

## 1964 Rickenbacker Capri Rose-Morris model 1993

**1. SERIAL NUMBER**
Two letters (denoting year and month of production) followed by two- or three-digit production number stamped on jack plate

**2. BODY**
1 ½-inch depth; semi-hollow; double-cutaway; unbound f-hole; solid glued-on back; non-contoured/flat top; tailpiece recess; bound top and back; Fireglo finish

**3. NECK**
Glued-on; dual truss rod system; 24 ¾-inch scale; three-piece (maple/walnut/maple) with walnut headstock wings; unbound rosewood fretboard with 21 frets and dot markers

**4. HARDWARE**
12 Kluson tuners; trapeze tailpiece; adjustable bridge; two metal strap-buttons

**5. PLASTICS**
Split-level white pickguard; white truss rod cover with black Rickenbacker logo and 'Made in U.S.A.' silkscreen; five black 'KK' knobs; black switch tip

**6. ELECTRONICS**
Dual 'toaster' single-coil pickups; three-way selector switch; independent pickup volume and tone pots; 'blend' pot; side-mounted jack

*Guitarist* would like to thank Martin Kelly and Paul Kelly, creators of *Rickenbacker Guitars: Out Of The Frying Pan Into The Fireglo* (Phantom Book) https://phantombooks.co

LEGENDARY GUITARS | 21

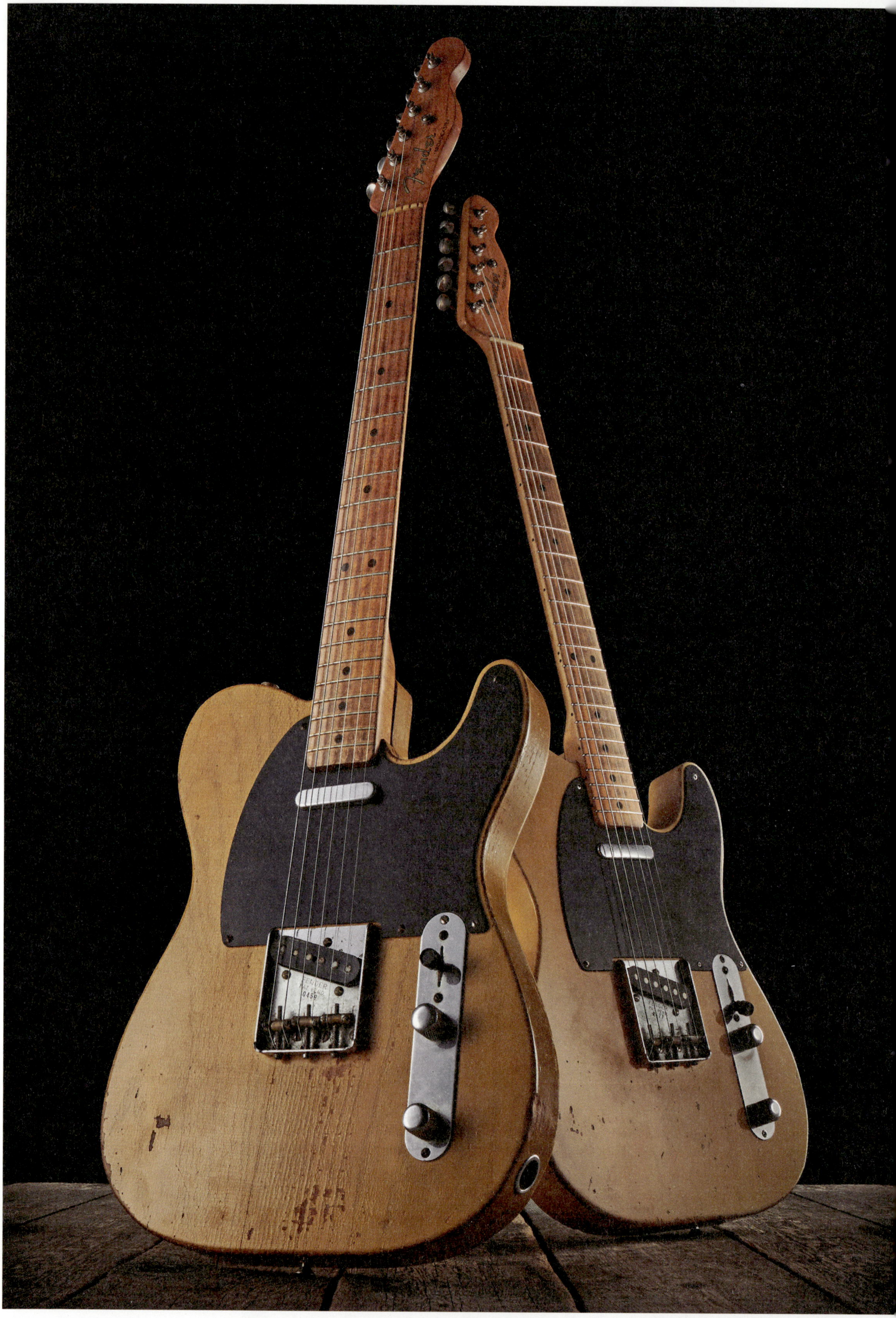
Fender

# THE FENDER
# TELECASTER
## *From Prototype To Present*

**FEW DESIGNS EVOLVE FROM PROTOTYPE TO SHOWROOM FLOOR IN JUST A COUPLE OF YEARS AND THEN GO ON TO REMAIN RELEVANT – AND, IN THEIR ESSENCE, UNCHANGED – FOR THE NEXT 70-PLUS YEARS. HERE, WE PAY TRIBUTE TO THE FIRST, AND JUST MAYBE THE GREATEST, SOLIDBODY ELECTRIC GUITAR: THE FENDER TELECASTER. JOIN US AS WE TRACE ITS EVOLUTION FROM SINGLE-PICKUP ESQUIRE ANCESTRY TO THE DEFINITIVE INCARNATION OF THIS AGELESS ELECTRIC**

**Words** Jamie Dickson & Rod Brakes  **Photography** Neil Godwin

The year is 1949. The Second World War had ended just four years previously but already a shining new technological age was beckoning. Jets streaked across the California skies – and down on terra firma, in Fullerton, California, Leo Fender was building the first prototypes of a guitar that would propel six-string design into the wide blue yonder.

These early testbed instruments were blocky, even crude looking. The body materials, pickups and control layout were experimental. But they had one pioneering feature that set them apart from every other guitar then available: a solid body. Even the name of this jet-age instrument was a kind of prototype back in '49. Leo planned to call it the Esquire, but – as we shall see – the guitar would gain a pickup and change names twice before it assumed the historic moniker that became famous for the next 70-plus years: Telecaster.

One man who has researched the early evolution of Leo's first electric guitar in forensic detail is David Davidson, co-owner of Well Strung Guitars and former curator of the Songbirds Guitar Museum in Chattanooga, Tennessee. He says that the solidbody concept was born of Leo Fender's practical outlook and desire to carve out a niche for himself in a guitar market that was still dominated by the old guard of tradition-steeped American guitar makers such as Gibson and Martin.

"Leo had been thinking for a period of time about coming up with an inexpensive alternative to the very expensive Gibson and Gretsch models," David says. "He was laughed at when he came out with a solidbody instrument. Mostly because people thought, 'How could that possibly sound good?' But he was a pretty diligent guy who just kept on trying to perfect it."

FEATURE | **Fender Telecaster: From Prototype To Present**

*Custom Shop recreation of the 'Snake Head' Esquire prototype of 1949*

Even in 1949, Fender had a few successes under his belt that suggested a solidbody electric might be the way forward. He'd launched a range of wooden-cabinet valve amplifiers including the Princeton, Deluxe and Professional the year after the war ended. These were designed for the electric lap-steel players of the era's country bands. He'd also built a twin-neck steel guitar for Noel Boggs of Bob Wills' Texas Playboys Western swing band – a huge act that played to 10,000 people every week. This had a slab-like horizontal body supported by legs, like a table. But despite its dissimilarity to a conventional guitar, it – and the range of multi-neck electric Fender lap steels that followed – offered compelling evidence that stringed solidbody electric instruments not only worked but sounded great and were well-liked by the musicians who used them. Crucially, Leo's clients on the country music scene provided a ready-made focus group helping him to design and refine his next and boldest innovation – a conventional 'Spanish' guitar with a solid body that made use of the lap-steel technology he'd been perfecting since 1946.

"He used his core group of local talent players to bounce instruments off," David Davidson explains. "He experimented with parts that were basically lap-steel parts in the beginning: pickups and such. And he experimented with different types of wood, primarily pine. He also experimented with chambered bodies and solid bodies to try and find the right combination. He would use everybody, from Rex Gallion to Bill Carson and other local players, to go out and experiment with these guitars. Sometimes he'd gift those guitars onto those people; sometimes he'd modify them many, many times over and hand them back out again to be used, until he could come up with what he thought was the perfect formula.

"The guitar takes shape in drawings in 1948, and becomes a guitar, a working specimen, in 1949. It would be hard for me to nail down a date and, in fact, you can only date [the earliest prototypes] by pot dates; they weren't putting neck dates on these guitars yet. The earliest pot date I have is a late-1948 pot date, but I'm sure the guitar itself was put together in 1949. We really don't know exactly when, because there are no other markings inside these guitars. They weren't up to that level of production."

> "Leo Fender was laughed at when he came out with a solidbody instrument… People thought, 'How could that possibly sound good?' But he was a diligent guy and kept trying to perfect it"
> **DAVID DAVIDSON**

### EARLY EVOLUTION

The early prototypes of what Leo initially dubbed the Esquire had a single pickup and these experimental builds tell a story of a guitar that evolved quickly from a rather crude initial design. As successive versions were built, the nascent 'Esquire' soon acquired hallmarks of Telecaster design DNA that we can recognise today.

"There's kind of an evolution that takes place, from the so-called 'Snake Head' guitar, which everyone's fairly familiar with, that had three tuners on each side of the headstock and a small pickguard. And that guitar was joined by a couple of cousins that have six-tuners-to-a-side headstocks. There is one that is stripped down to its original finish, pine, and then there was one with a pine body, six-on-a-side headstock, small pickguard, controls perpendicular to the neck… and that guitar is white. The original finish was an opaque white finish. The translucent blonde came later, after experimenting with different things."

As well as the basic outline of the guitar, the electronics and switching system was also revised several times as the guitar, still named the Esquire, neared readiness.

"At the museum we acquired the actual Esquire that appeared in the catalogue, which Leo shot himself. He was kind of a photo buff, so he actually photographed the guitar with the case and the strap himself. It's a very famous photo that's in the 1950 Fender catalogue, introducing the electric Spanish guitar. That guitar has

Leo Fender was tenacious in his search for the right sound and design, and sent his prototypes out into the wild to be test-driven by local guitar talent

LEO FENDER
PRESIDENT

Fender
ELECTRIC
INSTRUMENT
COMPANY, INC.

500 SOUTH RAYMOND AVE.
FULLERTON, CALIFORNIA
TELEPHONE: LA 6-5525

FEATURE | **Fender Telecaster**

> *"It took years for Gibson to get the Les Paul right, but Leo basically modelled himself after Henry Ford. Whatever the prototype is, the [production] guitar is going to be really close"*
> **DAVID DAVIDSON**

unique features, which are not featured on other instruments. One of them is that they had yet to come up with the idea for the three-way switch. So this guitar has a push-button switch, which is actually just a regular Leviton lamp switch that he would have picked up at Fullerton Hardware and installed in the guitar. And the control cavity is still shorter than what would become the production Esquire/Broadcaster. We call it the Lamp Switch Guitar."

It says something of the haste with which Leo wished to bring the Esquire to market that some of its features were provisional and would change further before the guitar was available for sale in earnest.

"That guitar is an ash body, but it's sandwiched together like some of the pine-body prototypes," David says. "It's probably one of the first – if not the very first – ash-body guitar. But it has a pancake body and, interestingly enough, it has a white pickguard made of fibreglass. I think they were experimenting with materials. This is before they made the decision to go with Bakelite on the guitar. They were probably weighing different things in the prototype stage. They simply laid out several layers of fibreglass matting and cut it to shape and attached it with five screws.

"There is no decal on the headstock, and the reason for that is if you look at the original catalogue photograph of the guitar, the word 'Fender' is actually an artist rendering in the photograph, so the Fender name is made larger and bolder in the photograph, but it's not on the guitar. It's also a no-truss-rod guitar. The pot dates to late 1948. The serial number is 0075, which is interesting because it was most likely made after the twin-pickup prototype number nine that I have, the red one, which is a pine body and has a lap steel pickup in the neck cavity. So that's an early piece in itself. I think he was just trying to get it right, you know? Where the pine body prototype is super, super light, it didn't have the same sustain as the ash body."

*A one-off Sunburst twin-pickup 'double Esquire' built in 1950 for early adopter Verlin Whitford*

## FROM ESQUIRE TO BROADCASTER

David's mention of twin-pickup prototypes ushers in the start of the modern Telecaster story. While the Esquire would be produced for many years in single-pickup format, it was clear early on that many musicians wanted more tonal variety than the standard Esquire's brash bridge pickup could provide. And so, ever keen to give musicians what they wanted, Leo soon began manufacturing twin-pickup versions of the Esquire. Mike Lewis of Fender's Custom Shop takes up the story…

"Fender made single-pickup versions and double-pickup versions of Esquires. So there were some early 1950 'double' Esquires that were, to all intents and purposes, what would later be called a Broadcaster and then a Telecaster, except it said 'Esquire' on the headstock at first. Possibly, when the single-pickup Esquire hit the market, people said, 'Hey, this is great, but we want two pickups.' So Leo makes them with two pickups as well. Then they're out there trying to sell this guitar and somebody says, 'Well, which is it? One pickup or two?' Maybe it got confusing. So they discontinued the 'double' Esquire and reintroduced it as a twin-pickup guitar called the Broadcaster. In fact, the double Esquire actually pre-dates the Broadcaster."

It was a lightning-fast development, but because it was guided by extensive developmental feedback from musicians, it's remarkable how many features of the twin-pickup Broadcaster model of 1950 have carried through to present-day Teles.

"It took years for Gibson to get the Les Paul right," says David Davidson of Well Strung Guitars, "but Leo Fender basically modelled himself after Henry Ford. Whatever the prototype is, the [production] guitar is going to be really

PHOTOGRAPHY BY JOBY SESSIONS

**Fender Telecaster: From Prototype To Present** | FEATURE

This 1953 Fender Esquire from ATB Guitars is testimony to the survival of the original single-pickup design into the Tele era

## THE EVOLUTION OF THE FENDER TELECASTER

### 1949
Leo Fender and George Fullerton complete the 'Snake Head' prototype solidbody electric guitar

### SPRING 1950
Single-pickup Esquire model first appears; dual-pickup Esquire built

### AUTUMN 1950
Dual-pickup Broadcaster with black 'guard, 'butterscotch' blonde finish and brass saddles released

### 1951
Broadcaster name dropped; Telecaster born

### 1954
White plastic pickguard; off-white blonde finish; steel bridge saddles

### 1955
Staggered bridge pickup polepieces

### 1958
'Top loading' bridge replaces 'string-through body' type; shallower neck

### 1959
'String-through body' bridge reintroduced; slab rosewood fretboards introduced

### 1969
Optional maple-cap 'board discontinued; fretted maple necks reintroduced

---

close to that prototype. Leo's research proved to be correct."

Nonetheless, Mike Lewis of Fender's Custom Shop says that the details of the early Broadcasters wandered around a little as Fender strove to settle on a definitive spec, yielding some early quirks that are still being rediscovered – and enjoyed – today.

"Some of those early, early Blackguards have a 7¼- to 9½-inch radius: what I call a 'vintage compound radius'. It either got that way over the years of being refretted, or maybe they didn't have the right tooling and jigs to begin with and it was done by hand, you know? The early pickups also had larger diameter magnets in many cases. For example, the bridge pickup in the early guitars sometimes had a .195 diameter magnet as opposed to a .187. The Double Esquire [reissue] in our Vintage Custom series is really that: it has a 7¼- to 9½-inch radius and those pickups with the larger magnets and the wiring. It's really cool."

The final stage in the development of the Esquire prototype into the Telecaster proper is well documented but bears repetition here. Perhaps nettled by the success of Fender's all-new solidbody, Gretsch lodged a complaint about the name Broadcaster, on the basis that it sold a drum kit named the Broadkaster. The chance of confusing the two products might seem remote, but as a fledgling company, Fender elected to avoid any possible legal entanglements by taking the Broadcaster decal off the headstocks of its production guitars for a period during 1951. Guitars made during this interregnum are today dubbed 'Nocasters' due to the absence of a formal model name. Finally, later that year, Fender renamed its twin-pickup single-cut the Telecaster – and a legend was born. **G**

LEGENDARY GUITARS | 27

*Electric*Evolution

# Fender Telecaster Custom (version 1)
### Fender's first foray into Telecaster variants was an upmarket alternative

The pictured Telecaster Custom was expertly restored to original spec at ATB Guitars in Cheltenham. By analysing the woodgrain, finish and other details such as neck date and pot codes, the team concluded it is the same prototypical instrument that appeared in Fender literature when the model was released in 1959. Reads the '59 catalogue: "The new Telecaster Custom dual pickup and Esquire Custom single pickup guitar offer all the fine playing and design features of the regular Telecaster and Esquire models plus custom treatment of the body and neck."

Costing $229.50, the Custom Telecaster was touted as a fancier, upmarket alternative to the plain, utilitarian design of the regular $199.50 Tele. This "custom treatment" included a rosewood 'board, three-ply pickguard, bound body, and three-tone sunburst finish. Appearing in '58, the top-of-the-line Jazzmaster was the first Fender solidbody to debut with a rosewood fretboard as standard, followed by the Telecaster and Esquire Customs. However, these models were not outstanding in this respect as one-piece fretted maple necks were superseded by rosewood-'board necks across the entire Fender line in '59. How rosewood 'boards compare with maple in terms of sound and feel will be debated ad infinitum, but they certainly tend to maintain their looks for longer, being darker in colour and lacquer-free.

Interestingly, some really early rosewood-'board necks, like the one pictured, have a walnut truss-rod plug and 'skunk stripe' as per the fretted maple necks. This guitar also features an ash body in the style of the regular/Blonde Teles, but such examples are very rare with alder being standard for Custom Teles and Esquires. Again, the effect on sound and feel/vibration is up for debate, but it's an important distinction.

The very earliest Telecaster Customs had a regular Telecaster headstock decal, but within months they were sporting a bespoke "Custom Telecaster" version. Somewhat confusingly, Fender simultaneously referred to the model as a "Telecaster Custom". When the black CBS-era headstock logo appeared in '67, the decal reverted to just "Telecaster". Several other important design alterations happened around that time, including the introduction of chrome-plated 'F' logo tuners and a matching neckplate. But the most significant change in terms of sound arrived with a new circuit configuration that facilitated all three pickup combinations along with full tone

> The most significant change in terms of sound arrived with a new circuit configuration

control for each. From '67 onwards, Fender listed prices for expanded options – notably a Fender/Bigsby vibrato and maple 'board (though it was possible to custom-order a guitar with a maple 'board prior to this).

Harder wearing poly finishes began to replace nitro around '68, and by 1970 the one-piece fretted maple neck had returned. By now, the Tele blueprint had been further developed in several different directions, with Mahogany, Rosewood, Paisley Red, Blue Flower and Thinline Teles joining the range. In '71, Fender introduced the Seth Lover-designed Wide Range humbucker by revamping the Thinline with a dual set. Prior to this, all Teles shared identical electronics. Following suit, the original Telecaster Custom design gave way to a non-bound, four-knob, single-coil/humbucker combo guitar in '72 (this second version has a stacked "Telecaster Custom" decal). The dual Wide Range 'bucker Telecaster Deluxe solidbody topped the Tele price list from '73.

*Although Fender experimented with 'top-loader' Tele bridges for a short time between '58 and '59, this guitar has been drilled for through-body stringing*

## The Evolution of the Fender Telecaster Custom

**1950**
Esquire & Broadcaster released; ash body; fretted maple neck; blonde finish; single-layer pickguard

**1951**
Dual-pickup Broadcaster renamed Telecaster

**Mid-1959**
Telecaster & Esquire Customs released; bound alder body; rosewood fretboard; 3-tone sunburst finish

**Summer 1959**
3-ply 5-screw pickguard changes to 3-ply 8-screw type

**1962**
Slab rosewood fretboard changes to veneer

**1963/'64**
Maroon sides (preceded and superseded by black)

**1967**
Circuit changes to standard 3-way switching with full tone control

**Late 1960s**
"Fender/Bigsby Tremolo" and maple fingerboard options listed

**1970**
Fretted maple necks optional; Esquire Custom discontinued

**1972**
Telecaster Custom discontinued; Telecaster Custom version 2 released

*Electric*Evolution

## Fender Telecaster Custom (version 1)

**1. SERIAL NUMBER**
Five-digit number stamped onto neckplate in '58/'59 (though Fender prototypes often have no serial number)

**2. HEADSTOCK**
Metal string tree; 'spaghetti' Fender logo and "Telecaster" decal; walnut truss-rod plug

**3. PLASTICS**
Three-layer (w/b/w), five-screw pickguard (repro); black switch tip

**4. HARDWARE**
'Single-line' Kluson Deluxe tuners; steel bridge plate ('top-loader' standard from late '58 to late '59); three threaded adjustable saddles; two metal strap buttons. Chrome-plated: front pickup cover; 'ashtray' bridge cover; control plate; two knurled knobs; recessed side jack

**5. PICKUPS**
Two 'black bottom' single-coil pickups; three-way selector switch; two CTS pots (volume and tone); Telecaster circuit from 1953 to 1967 featured: neck with 'bass' preset /no tone (position 3); neck with tone (position 2); and bridge with tone (position 1)

**6. BODY**
Solid ash (alder standard); single-cutaway; three-tone sunburst nitrocellulose finish (wider than standard); bound top and back

**7. NECK**
Bolt-on; one-piece maple; walnut 'skunk stripe'; slab rosewood fretboard; 21 frets; 'clay' dot markers; nitrocellulose clearcoat finish; dated '10/58' (Oct 1958)

With thanks to ATB Guitars
www.atbguitars.com

**DAZED & CONFUSED**

# CBS FENDER TELECASTERS

Custom Telecaster or Telecaster Custom?
We clear up the confusion on CBS-era Teles

The Telecaster has appeared in many different guises since the basic design went to market in 1950. Fender's first solidbody electric guitar, the single (bridge) pickup Esquire, was introduced during spring 1950, while the odd dual-pickup Esquire was made that summer. Fender decided to launch these dual-pickup instruments separately as the Broadcaster in autumn 1950, though following a trademark disagreement with Gretsch they were rebranded Telecaster in 1951. This landmark electric has now been in production for over seven decades.

The Telecaster continued to evolve throughout the 50s, transitioning away from the original Blackguard livery in 1954 with a lighter blonde finish and white pickguard. The model's greatest change would come in 1959 when rosewood fingerboards became standard across the Fender line. In June that year, the Esquire and Telecaster Custom models appeared, their bound bodies resplendent in a three-tone sunburst finish and topped with a three-ply (w/b/w) nitrate pickguard. These instruments marked Fender's first foray away from the traditional 'plain Jane' design.

As the 60s progressed, bigger changes were afoot at Fender as a whole, and by 1965 the brand was firmly in the hands of its new owners CBS. For better or worse, the corporate giant was less bound by tradition and soon began to take the humble Tele into areas previously unimagined. **G**

*Guitarist* would like to thank ATB Guitars in Cheltenham and Adrian Hornbrook

## 1 TELECASTER THINLINE

In 1962, pioneering guitar designer Roger Rossmeisl departed fellow Californian guitar builder Rickenbacker to join Fender. After helping launch the firm's acoustic guitar range in 1963, he moved on to develop the semi-hollowbody electric Coronado design in early 1966 before beginning work on a hollow Telecaster design the following year. With its non-contoured body, the Tele proved an ideal testbed for such experimentation, and by 1968 Rossmeisl and his assistant, Virgilio Simoni, had refined a method of construction for a new Telecaster model.

Launched in 1968, the Telecaster Thinline initially came in either a natural ash or mahogany finish; a three-tone sunburst option became available later in the year. In 1971, the standard Telecaster pickup configuration was superseded by dual Wide Range humbuckers designed by father of the Gibson PAF, Seth Lover. The model remained in production throughout the 1970s until it was pulled from the catalogue at the end of the decade.

## 2 PAISLEY RED & BLUE FLOWER TELECASTERS

Equally striking a departure from the traditional Telecaster design were the Paisley Red and Blue Flower Teles that appeared in limited numbers in 1968. With Fender hoping to connect with the zeitgeist of flower power, these two markedly psychedelic finishes were achieved by using a peel-and-stick product made by the Borden Chemical company called Cling-Foil. This aluminium foil (effectively a thick metallic wallpaper) was fixed to the wood before being blown over around the body edges and pickup routs.

"Paisley Red pulsates with every beat and swirls in a blinding carousel of colour forms and tones. Fender shines again," says an advert for the Paisley Red Telecaster. Its Blue Flower counterpart reads: "Blue Flower bursts forth in a dazzling array of subtle purple and green patterns. Never before has such an exciting profusion of colour been offered." Unfortunately, many of these rare Teles suffered from severe fading and checking.

## 3 TELECASTER CUSTOM

While the original dual-single-coil/sunburst Telecaster Custom was discontinued in 1972, that same year a radically overhauled design appeared. Advertised as the Telecaster Custom (though often referred to as the "Custom Telecaster"), the new model sported the unique configuration of a regular Tele-style single-coil bridge pickup along with a Wide Range humbucker in the neck position. Featuring Les Paul-style controls, including independent pickup volume and tone pots and a three-way switch on the upper bass bout, the newly designed 'version two' Telecaster Custom offered players a unique combination of sounds that covered both Gibson and Fender territory.

From 1973, with the introduction of the dual-'bucker Telecaster Deluxe, three out of four of Fender's Tele designs carried the new Wide Range pickup; only the standard Tele retained its existing dual single coils. This latter version of the Telecaster Custom was discontinued in 1981 (along with the Telecaster Deluxe).

## 4 TELECASTER DELUXE

As hard rock became more popular during the late 60s and early 70s, new Tele designs evolved in order to meet demand while existing models fell by the wayside. By 1970, both the Esquire and Esquire Custom guitars were discontinued, followed by the original/sunburst Telecaster Custom and the George Harrison-endorsed Rosewood Telecaster in '72. The Telecaster Deluxe made its debut soon after in '73, hoping to compete with Gibson's Les Paul Standard directly with a dual-humbucker-loaded guitar.

Like its contemporary Telecaster Custom model, the hybrid-design Telecaster Deluxe features Les Paul-style controls and a large scratchplate. In addition, it has a CBS-era Stratocaster-style wide headstock, "micro-neck-adjust" three-bolt neckplate system, and 'belly cut' rear contour. Early on, the Telecaster Deluxe was also offered with a Strat-style "tremolo" option. Larger frets and a 9.5-inch radius complete its unique feel. It remained at the top of the Telecaster price list throughout its production.

1

2

3

4

*Electric*Evolution

# 1950s Fender Stratocasters

Launched in the 50s, Fender's iconic solidbody soon reached the heights of success

Aside from their fretted maple necks, 1950s Fender Stratocasters can be identified by either a two-tone sunburst (comprising dark brown and yellow) or, from '58, a three-tone sunburst. Unfortunately, the red aniline dye used in these later finishes tended to fade severely, much like the 'Bursts/Les Paul Standards of the time. Consequently, many late-50s Strats are misconstrued as having a two-tone finish. However, by 1960, Fender had addressed this issue (as had Gibson) and, from that point onwards, Strats were endowed with a more stable and bolder-looking sunburst.

Released in 1954, the Stratocaster was the first of Fender's 'electric Spanish' solidbodies to feature a sunburst finish as standard. Its existing models, released earlier in 1950 – namely the Esquire and the Telecaster, which was originally known as the Broadcaster – came with a transparent blonde finish that showed off the figuring of the ash body underneath. Strats were similarly constructed using ash up until mid-1956 when they switched to alder (aside from Strats finished in blonde, which could be ordered for a five per cent upcharge). With their semi-transparent two-tone sunbursts and figured ash bodies, these early Strats (such as the 1954 example pictured opposite) have a distinctive look that immediately dates them to within the first couple of years of production.

The Stratocaster featured a versatile triple-pickup configuration and bespoke vibrato system, and was conceived as a replacement for the "plain Jane" Telecaster, while serving to compete directly with Gibson's Les Paul Model (released in 1952). Work on the Tele's successor started as early as 1951, but it would be a few years before Leo Fender felt the design was ready to take to market. While Leo was not a seasoned guitarist, through close collaboration with several professional musicians during the design process – notably Rex Gallion, Bill Carson and Freddie Tavares – he was able to realise an instrument that ultimately became not just a classic guitar but also a bona fide icon of popular culture.

As per its predecessor, the Telecaster, it is often said that 'Leo got it right the first time' with the Stratocaster. And it's hard to argue against that sentiment. As opposed to the Les Paul, both have remained in production ever since they appeared during America's colourful post-war years and their essential blueprints have stayed the same. The majority of the changes Fender implemented on the Strat were cosmetic in nature, while aiming to produce a harder-wearing and better-looking guitar. For example, it was noted the polystyrene pickup covers and knobs were prone to breakage and so these were superseded by a tougher ABS plastic during '57. A similar change happened in '59 when the Strat's white single-layer plastic pickguard was replaced by a three-layer (white/black/white) nitrate type.

The most prominent change also occurred in '59 when rosewood fretboards were implemented across Fender's entire range following the introduction of the Jazzmaster the previous year. Unlike lacquered maple, rosewood didn't appear markedly discoloured with wear, and many preferred the new look overall. It marked the end of an era, but it also signalled the beginning of an exciting new time for the Fender Stratocaster. **G**

## The Evolution of the Fender Stratocaster – 1954–1960

### 1951
Work on the Telecaster's successor commences

### Late 1953
Synchronized Tremolo vibrato system design completed

### April 1954
Earliest known Stratocaster (serial number 0100)

### October 1954
Full-scale production; ash body; 2-tone sunburst; white single-ply pickguard; round string-tree

### 1955
Sharper headstock edges; chunky neck profile retained; c.450 shipped (c.70% increase on 1954)

### 1956
Alder body (excluding blonde finish); butterfly string tree; V-profile neck

### 1957
Transition from polystyrene to ABS plastic parts; V-profile neck

### 1958
3-tone sunburst; slimmer neck profile

### 1959
'Slab' (flat base) rosewood fingerboard; 3-ply (w/b/w) nitrate pickguard

### 1960
Fade-resistant red/ bolder 3-tone sunburst

32 | LEGENDARY GUITARS

*Electric*Evolution

## 1954 Fender Stratocaster

**1. SERIAL NUMBER**
0146; impressed into backplate and stamped in black

**2. HEADSTOCK**
Stauffer/Bigsby-style profile; rounded edges; decals read 'Fender Stratocaster with Synchronized Tremolo' and 'Original Contour Body'; nitrocellulose clearcoat

**3. BODY**
Ash; double-cutaway; rounded edges; forearm and belly contours; two-tone sunburst nitrocellulose finish

**4. PICKUPS**
Three height-adjustable single-coil 'floating' pickups; master volume pot; neck pickup tone pot; middle pickup tone pot; one tone capacitor; three-way selector switch; front-loading jack socket

**5. HARDWARE**
Six nickel-plated Kluson 'no line' tuners; round metal string-tree; Synchronized Tremolo vibrato system with six fully adjustable saddles; two metal strap buttons; chrome-plated: jack plate, neckplate, detachable vibrato arm and 'ash tray' bridge cover (arm and cover not pictured)

**6. PLASTICS**
White single-layer pickguard with eight screw holes; three white pickup covers with rubber spacers; three white control knobs (one 'volume' and two 'tone'); white switch tip; white vibrato arm tip; white backplate with six screw and six string holes

**7. NECK**
Single-piece fretted maple; bolt-on (four screws); 21 frets; black dot markers; 25½-inch scale length; adjustable truss rod; walnut 'skunk stripe' and headstock plug; bone nut; nitrocellulose clearcoat

*Guitarist* would like to thank Vintage 'n' Rare Guitars in Bath for showing us this stunning example

*Electric*Evolution

# 1960s Fender Stratocasters

The Strat continues its journey towards iconic status as a new decade unfolds

By the beginning of the 1960s, the Stratocaster had already experienced its most significant changes. In 1959, rosewood fretboards with 'clay' dot markers superseded the guitar's initial fretted maple-neck design, and an 11-hole, three-layer 'mint green' nitrate pickguard replaced the original eight-hole, single-layer white plastic 'guard.

The first rosewood fretboards had a flat base and are thus referred to as 'slab' fretboards. Slab 'boards can be easily identified at either end of the neck, exhibiting a downwards curve at the headstock. In August 1962, Fender began using a curved-base veneer rosewood fretboard, which became thinner the following year. Contrary to slab 'boards, veneer 'boards display an upwards curve at the headstock end.

By 1960, Fender had addressed the issue of fading that occurred with the red aniline layer of its three-tone sunburst finish introduced earlier in 1958 (prior to this, Strats came with a two-tone dark brown/yellow sunburst as standard). By 1961, the dark brown outer layer became even darker giving the finish a somewhat bolder look overall. The sunburst changed appearance yet again in 1964 when Fender began spraying the bodies yellow in addition to using a yellow dip-dye. These vibrant 'target burst' finishes appear more opaque and are therefore better able to mask visual imperfections in the guitar's alder body.

In 1961, Fender introduced its first custom-colour chart, enabling customers to order a Stratocaster in their choice of 14 different shades in addition to Blond and the standard sunburst finish. These DuPont automotive paint colours included: Daphne Blue, Sonic Blue, Black, Sherwood Green Metallic, Foam Green, Surf Green, Fiesta Red, Dakota Red and Shell Pink nitrocellulose/Duco, along with Lake Placid Blue Metallic, Shoreline Gold Metallic, Olympic White, Burgundy Mist Metallic and Inca Silver Metallic acrylic/Lucite. Custom colours worked a treat to help popularise the Strat, and sales steadily increased throughout the decade.

Also, in '61, the Strat's neck profile became thicker (albeit not as chunky as the rounded- and V-profile neck guitars made between '54 and '58). From this point onwards, Strats retained an approximation of a modern C-profile, with relatively minor changes occurring throughout the 60s. The same year, two patent number decals appeared on the headstock, increasing to five by 1965. In 1964, a thicker gold/black outlined 'transition' logo replaced the original thin 'spaghetti' logo. Late the following year, the Strat's headstock was widened and a couple of years after that was adorned with a new black/gold outlined CBS-designed Fender logo, which appeared alongside an enlarged model name decal featuring solid black block lettering.

By 1968, Fender began using polyester finishes as a way of speeding up production and sustaining its instruments' clean appearance for longer. In the automotive industry, nitrocellulose lacquer had largely been replaced by more stable, harder-wearing materials by then, and Fender moved with the times. These thicker finishes changed the look and feel of the Strat – and many will argue the sound of it, too – although this didn't slow down the momentum of rock 'n' roll in the slightest, as the era of hard rock really got underway. Indeed, Hendrix almost single handedly elevated the Strat to unprecedented levels of popularity – poly finishes and funky flared headstocks or not. **G**

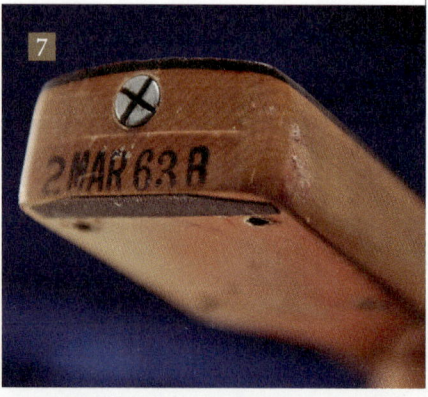

## The Evolution of the Fender Stratocaster 1960-1969

**1960**
5-digit serial numbers; black-bottom pickups; formvar coil wire; 'spaghetti' logo

**1961**
Headstock patent numbers; thicker C-profile neck

**1962**
Brazilian rosewood veneer fretboard; L-prefixed serial number (late '62)

**1963**
Thinner fretboard veneer; pickguard screw adjacent to middle pickup

**1964**
Grey-bottom pickups; enamel coil wire; 'transition' logo (gold/black outline); pearloid dots

**1965**
New pickguard plastic; 'F'-stamped neckplate, 6-digit serial number & flared headstock (late '65)

**1966**
'F' logo tuners (most still with 'double-line' Kluson Deluxe brand); Indian rosewood fretboard

**1967**
Optional maple fretboard advertised; CBS logo (black/gold outline); large model name decal

**1968**
Polyester finishes

**1969**
9 remaining custom colour options (including Blond)

*Electric*Evolution

## 1963 Fender Stratocaster in Fiesta Red

**1. SERIAL NUMBER**
89479; stamped on neckplate

**2. HEADSTOCK**
Stauffer/Bigsby-style profile; decals read 'Fender Stratocaster with Synchronized Tremolo' and 'Original Contour Body'; three patent numbers; nitrocellulose clearcoat

**3. BODY**
Alder; double-cutaway; rounded edges; forearm and belly contours; Fiesta Red nitrocellulose finish

**4. PICKUPS**
Three height-adjustable single-coil 'floating' pickups; master volume pot; neck pickup tone pot; middle pickup tone pot; one tone capacitor; three-way selector switch; front-loading jack socket

**5. HARDWARE**
Six nickel-plated 'single-line' Kluson Deluxe tuners; 'butterfly' metal string tree; Synchronized Tremolo vibrato system with six fully adjustable saddles; two metal strap buttons; chrome-plated: jack plate, neckplate, detachable vibrato arm and 'ash tray' bridge cover

**6. PLASTICS**
Three-layer (w/b/w) 'mint green' cellulose nitrate pickguard with 11 screw holes; three white pickup covers with rubber spacers; three white control knobs (one 'volume' and two 'tone'); white switch tip; white vibrato arm tip; white backplate

**7. NECK**
Single-piece fretted maple; bolt-on (four screws); 25½-inch scale length; Brazilian rosewood veneer fretboard; 21 frets; 'clay' dot markers; adjustable truss rod; bone nut; stamped '2MAR63B' on heel; nitrocellulose clearcoat

*Guitarist* would like to thank Vintage 'n' Rare Guitars in Bath (www.vintageandrareguitars.com)

LEGENDARY GUITARS | *35*

*Electric*Evolution

# Fender Jazzmaster

Fender's original offset solidbody makes a splash in the surf and new wave scenes…

By the late 50s Fender had established itself as a force to be reckoned with. Often seen in the hands of guitarists across a range of genres from blues and country to rock 'n' roll, the company's Telecaster (introduced as the Broadcaster in 1950) and Stratocaster (released in 1954) were proving popular, although they were seldom adopted among jazz players.

The booming electric jazz guitar scene of the 1950s was dominated by Gibson's ES (Electric Spanish) series, with its flagship Super 400CES and L-5CES electric archtops setting formidably high standards. It was an area of the market Fender was keen to tap into, but rather than trying to beat Gibson at its own game by building electric semi/hollowbody instruments, it decided to take the equally ambitious tack of developing an all-new electric solidbody design.

Aimed at jazz guitarists, the Jazzmaster model was prototyped during 1957 and then introduced in the following year at the top of Fender's price list. An early advertisement for the guitar reads: "The revolutionary offset waist body design offers the ultimate in playing comfort… playing is effortless," highlighting the sleek contours of Fender's new solidbody in an attempt to steer the market's attention away from its competitors' bulkier and old-fashioned archtops.

Untried and untested, however, the Jazzmaster was so different to the likes of Gibson and Epiphone's long-established benchmark designs that it never gained mass appeal in the jazz world.

Perhaps the only feature that appeared to be borrowed from the competition was the Jazzmaster's rosewood fingerboard – a first

## The Jazzmaster was so different to other designs that it never gained mass appeal in the jazz world

for Fender. It was a striking new addition that didn't appear to wear as noticeably as Fender's existing lacquered, fretted maple necks and, by 1959, rosewood fretboards had become standard on all models across the range, including the Esquire, Telecaster, Stratocaster and Precision Bass.

Finished in Fender's new three-tone sunburst as standard, the Jazzmaster came equipped with a unique 'Tremolo' system that would also later appear on the similarly 'offset' body Jaguar (released in 1962). Consisting of a spring-loaded tailpiece and floating bridge, this mechanism has a notably smooth and gentle action, and when used with the relatively heavier gauges of string that were popular at the time of its design (0.012-gauge and above), it proves remarkably stable.

With the typically warmer tones of the jazz guitarist in mind and to further distinguish the Jazzmaster from its predecessors, Fender developed a new dual set of single-coil pickups with wide, flat coils that produced a thicker, more rounded sound. A two-position slide switch located on the upper bass bout enables a 'preset' selection of either the single/front pickup 'rhythm' circuit or the dual-pickup 'lead' circuit. Two roller pots control the volume and tone of the rhythm circuit, while a regular three-way pickup selector switch along with standard tone and volume knobs are assigned to the lead circuit.

Despite being largely ignored by jazz guitarists following its arrival, the Jazzmaster found a much wider stylistic appeal than its name implies. Bob Bogle, Tom Verlaine, Elvis Costello, Robert Smith, Kevin Shields and J Mascis are all known to favour the Jazzmaster. Even Jimi Hendrix was known to strap one on from time to time (upside down, of course!).

*The earlier models featured Fender's 'spaghetti' logo*

*The Jazzmaster came with a unique 'Tremolo' system complete with a floating bridge*

## 1959 Fender Jazzmaster

**1. SERIAL NUMBER**
Five-digit number (typically between 34000-43000) stamped into neck plate

**2. HEADSTOCK**
Flared Stratocaster-style profile; gold 'spaghetti' Fender logo; nitrocellulose clearcoat finish

**3. BODY**
Two-piece solid alder; offset profile; rib and forearm contours; three-tone sunburst nitrocellulose finish

**4. PICKUPS**
Two wide/flat single-coil pickups; two-position lead/rhythm circuit slide switch; 1meg-ohms volume and 50kohms tone roller pots (rhythm circuit); three-way pickup selector toggle switch, volume, tone 1meg-ohms pots (lead circuit); brass tray cavity shielding

**5. HARDWARE**
Gold-coloured aluminium pickguard; front-loading jack socket; single-line Kluson Deluxe tuners; butterfly string tree and spacer; chrome-plated top-loading spring-loaded tailpiece with lock switch and floating bridge 'Tremolo'; chrome-plated bridge cover; chrome-plated 'Tremolo' arm

**6. PLASTICS**
ABS pickup covers; ABS volume and tone knobs (lead circuit); rhythm/lead circuit switch grip; three-way pickup selector switch tip (lead circuit); 'Tremolo' arm tip

**7. NECK**
25½-inch scale length; one-piece solid maple; Brazilian rosewood 'slab' board; 21 frets; 'clay' dot markers; bone nut; 7¼-inch radius

*Guitarist* would like to thank Mike Long at ATB Guitars in Cheltenham (www.atbguitars.com)

---

## Electric Evolution

### The Evolution of the Fender Jazzmaster

**1958**
Fender Jazzmaster released; gold-coloured aluminium pickguard

**1959**
4-layer (w/b/w/tortoiseshell) or 3-layer (w/b/w) celluloid pickguard

**1962**
'Curved' Brazilian rosewood fingerboards replace 'slab' type

**1963**
Thinner 'veneer' Brazilian rosewood fingerboards

**1964**
Headstock decal changes from 'spaghetti' to 'transition' Fender logo

**1965**
Bound fretboard; enlarged headstock; metal cap skirt knobs replace Stratocaster-style knobs

**1966**
Pearloid block fretboard markers replace dot inlays

**1967**
Maple fingerboard with black block fretboard markers optional; black CBS Fender logo

**1968**
Polyester finish introduced

**1979**
Last appeared in Fender price list at $740 (omitted in 1980 price list)

LEGENDARY GUITARS | 37

*ElectricEvolution*

# Fender Jaguar

Riding the wave of 60s surf, the Jag topped Fender's big-game guitars…

Appearing in music stores in a striking range of custom colours in addition to the regular Sunburst finish, Jaguars first arrived in mid-1962 and topped the price list of Fender's solidbody electric guitar line at $379.50 – a major difference in cost at the time when compared with its $259.50 Stratocaster and $209.50 Telecaster. But Strats and Teles were the popular choice behind the burgeoning rock music scene of the mid to late 60s as far as Fenders go, and the Jaguar subsequently fell into relative obscurity.

Jaguars did, however, prove to be a popular choice for surf musicians in the early 60s – The Beach Boys' Carl Wilson being one notable player – and were generally marketed in order to appeal to the younger and apparently more adventurous generation. Early advertisements for the Jaguar show some impressive, albeit eye-watering, double tasking: one man is pictured playing a Jaguar while riding a surfboard, and another ad depicts a motocross rider in mid-air with a Jag strapped to his back!

Although inheriting some obvious similarities from Fender's second most expensive guitar at the time, the Jazzmaster (priced at $349.50), such as the 'tremolo' system and an offset body shape, Jaguars are markedly different in terms of sound and feel. Their 24-inch scale length – as opposed to the Jazzmaster's 25.5-inch scale length – is, in fact, more similar to Gibson's electric guitars. A bridge mute assembly installed on Jaguars as standard (although rarely used because it offered little control and often detuned the guitar) further sets the two instruments apart, while the Jaguar's unique 'saw-tooth' pickups produce a distinctively thinner, brighter and characteristically detailed tone. A 'strangle' switch located next to the pickup on/off switches on the control panel of the upper treble bout thins out the sound by way of engaging a capacitor/filter.

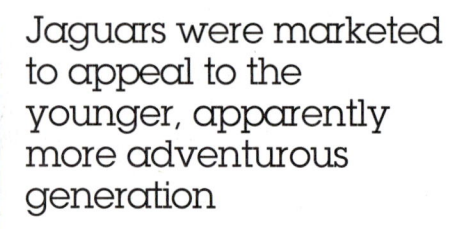

> **Jaguars were marketed to appeal to the younger, apparently more adventurous generation**

The Jaguar's 'lead' and 'rhythm' circuit controls are spread across three chrome panels and might appear somewhat busy or confusing at first, but they may simply be thought of as a means to instantly swap between the different volume and tone settings of the front pickup: the back pickup is disabled in 'rhythm' mode, and in 'lead' mode the ability to switch both pickups on or off independently is activated (with 'strangle' switch engage optional).

The Jaguar fell so far out of favour during the 60s and early 70s that in 1975 Fender discontinued it altogether. However, it became a guitar of choice for many, often leftfield players who later discovered its charms (including their relatively low price!) on the vintage market. Following the Jaguar's abandonment, Fender has since reintroduced its former flagship on several occasions due to an ever increasing demand, thanks in part to such notable guitarists as Marc Ribot, Tom Verlaine, Johnny Marr, Kurt Cobain and John Frusciante.

Nowadays, it seems as if there is a Jaguar model available for every player with Fender currently offering the guitar in a wide variety of pickup configurations and colour options across its Custom Shop, American Original, Artist, Player, Vintera and Squier ranges.

*This switch-laden '62 Jag was a real draw for the surf crowd of the 60s*

*Electric*Evolution

## 1962 'Green Sparkle' Fender Jaguar

**1. SERIAL NUMBER**
Five digits stamped into the neckplate

**2. HEADSTOCK**
Flared, matching headstock; solid black 'Jaguar' logo, Fender logo and 'Offset contour body' decal; single string tree

**3. PLASTICS**
Three-ply tortoiseshell celluloid pickguard; foam mute; 'lead' circuit controls on treble side: volume and tone knobs with independent pickup on/off and 'strangle' switches; 'rhythm' circuit controls on bass side: circuit selection switch (metal 'rhythm' circuit volume and tone roller knobs); white vinyl pickup covers

**4. HARDWARE**
Single line Deluxe Kluson tuners; 'PAT # 2,972,923' floating vibrato/'tremolo' system; 'Fender Mute' engraved mute control; adjustable six-saddle bridge; three chrome control panels

**5. PICKUPS**
Two Stratocaster-sized pickups with saw-tooth chrome pickup cradles (concentrates magnet field underneath string and reduces interference)

**6. BODY**
Solid alder body with Jazzmaster-style offset shape; ultra-rare 'Green Sparkle' finish (with matching headstock)

**7. NECK**
Bolt-on one-piece maple neck with thick Brazilian rosewood 'slab' fretboard and 'clay' dot markers; adjustable truss rod

## The Evolution Of The Fender Jaguar

**Mid 1962**
Jaguar introduced with thick 'slab' Brazilian rosewood fretboard, 'clay' dot inlays and flat pickup polepieces

**August 1962**
Veneer Brazilian rosewood fretboard

**1964**
Staggered pickup polepieces

**1965**
Bound fretboard and pearloid dot inlays

**1966**
Block fretboard inlays

**1967**
Kluson Deluxe branded tuners change to F-style and headstock Fender logo changes from black and gold to solid black

**1968**
Nitrocellulose finish changes to polyester

**1975**
Discontinued

**1986**
Japanese '62 reissue introduced

**1999**
American '62 reissue introduced

LEGENDARY GUITARS | 39

*Electric*Evolution

# Fender Electric XII

Fender chimes in with its answer to an electric 12-string…

The Electric XII may not be Fender's most popular or well-known guitar, but in terms of design it's one of the best 12-string electrics ever made. Easy to play, stable and with an impressive breadth of tone, they are one of the most usable instruments of their type. Although many people these days would be inclined to use a chorus pedal to conveniently simulate the tone of a 12-string, the natural complexity, shimmer and chime of multiple string courses is a wonderful sound that endures across various guitar-playing styles.

12-string acoustics were around for a long time before the advent of their electric siblings and became relatively popular after appearing in catalogues during the early 1900s. As inexpensive blues and folk instruments, they were adopted by some of the early guitar luminaries such as Blind Willie McTell and "King of the 12-String Guitar" Huddie 'Lead Belly' Ledbetter, while in later years 12-strings became a regular fixture of the 50s/60s folk boom. By this stage, electric solidbodies were well established and the concept migrated over to this more modern format, beginning with the Gibson Double 12/EDS-1275 and Danelectro Bellzouki.

It was Fender's fellow Californian builder Rickenbacker, however, that really brought the instrument to the fore in 1964 when George Harrison's prototype 360-12 appeared in The Beatles' film *A Hard Day's Night*. After that, Fender developed an electric 12-string model of its own in anticipation of a continued surge in demand, but they were never a huge seller and the Electric XII was produced for only a short time between '65 and '69.

Synonymous with mid-60s hits such as The Beatles' *Ticket To Ride* and The Byrds' *Mr Tambourine Man*, electric 12-strings are something of a secret weapon in the studio, with Eric Clapton, Pete Townshend and Jimmy Page all having used an Electric XII to record with. Soon after its release, Bob Dylan was photographed using a standard sunburst finish model during his '65 *Highway 61 Revisited* sessions (as pictured in

## Synonymous with mid-60s hits, electric 12-strings are something of a secret weapon in the studio

the album's artwork), while The Beach Boys' Carl Wilson was snapped the same year playing an Olympic White pre-production Electric XII. Custom colour Electric XIIs were produced in greater relative proportion to catch the eye of would-be buyers, with Olympic White, Candy Apple Red and Lake Placid Blue being among the more common.

With an offset body, the Electric XII follows the basic form of its predecessors the Jazzmaster, Jazz Bass, Bass VI and Jaguar, while its most distinguishing feature is undoubtedly the large six-a-side hockey stick-shaped headstock (as per the Fender Villager and Shenandoah 12-string acoustics, also released in '65).

Masterminded by Leo Fender, the Electric XII's 12-saddle bridge is a stroke of genius, providing full adjustment of each string for near-perfect intonation and action, while its string-through-body design and tight break angle enhances sustain. Two split pickups located in the bridge and neck positions provide expansive tonal options in conjunction with master tone and volume controls and a four-way switch (offering either individual, dual or out-of-phase operation).

## The Evolution of Fender 12-String Electrics

### June 1965
Electric XII solidbody released; standard sunburst finishes with white pearloid pickguard

### 1965
Sunburst with faux tortoiseshell pickguard; pearloid dot inlays

### Early 1966
Fender Coronado XII thinline introduced (final Antigua XII version discontinued 1973)

### Mid-1966
Electric XII with bound neck with block inlays (rare)

### 1969
Electric XII discontinued

### 1987-1990
Stratocaster XII

### 1993-1996
Strat XII

### 1995
Telecaster XII

### 2005-2009
Stratocaster XII

### 2019
Alternate Reality Series Electric XII

*Electric*Evolution

## 1965 Fender Electric XII in Firemist Gold

**1. SERIAL NUMBER**
F-series ('F' neckplate logo); six-digit serial number impressed into neckplate (usually 100000-110000 range for 1965)

**2. HEADSTOCK**
Large 'hockey stick' headstock; six-a-side tuners; matching Firemist Gold custom colour finish; decal reads 'Fender Electric XII'

**3. BODY**
Solid alder; offset contoured design; Firemist Gold custom colour finish

**4. PICKUPS & ELECTRICS**
Adjustable dual split pickups; four-way rotary selector switch (individual, together and out-of-phase operation); master volume and tone controls (two 1meg-ohms pots and 0.022uF ceramic 'pancake' tone capacitor); front-loading jack socket

**5. HARDWARE**
Chrome-plated: control panel; string-through-body bridge with 12 fully adjustable 'barrel' saddles; 12 individual 'F'-stamped tuners; string guide

**6. PLASTICS**
Three-ply (w/b/w) pickguard with bevelled edge; four black pickup covers; two black metal-capped Fender amp-style knobs; black selector switch

**7. NECK**
One-piece maple; bolt-on; 25½-inch scale length; 21-fret rosewood veneer fretboard with pearloid dot inlays; date-stamped 'OCT65'

*Guitarist* would like to thank ATB Guitars in Cheltenham for showing us this 1965 Fender Electric XII in Firemist Gold

LEGENDARY GUITARS | *41*

*Electric*Evolution

# Fender VI

Fender gets to third bass with a minor hit, the VI…

Nowadays, any sense of the exotic evoked by a Fender VI pales in comparison to how extraordinary Leo Fender's electric instruments were upon their debut. Today, solidbody electric guitars and basses are so embedded in our psyche that it's difficult to imagine where we might be without them, but prior to the 1950s, such technology was pretty revolutionary. It's a wonder that Fender managed to create a demand for such striking innovations at all, let alone change the face of popular culture with them. All the same, some designs proved to be more of an acquired taste than others.

The solidbody electric guitar as we know it today evolved from its acoustic ancestors via several developmental steps that were intended to increase the audibility of the instrument within a band, while its bass counterparts evolved in parallel from upright, fretless basses in a similar vein.

In the decade after Leo Fender introduced these groundbreaking guitars to the mass market – with the Esquire/Broadcaster in 1950 and the Precision Bass in 1951 – he continued to expand the company's catalogue and in 1960 released the Jazz Bass, which was followed shortly afterwards by the Fender VI (often referred to as the 'Bass Six') in 1961.

Sporting an offset body and floating vibrato system, the VI is immediately reminiscent of Fender's Jazzmaster, released a few years earlier in 1958, and came in sunburst with a tortoiseshell celluloid pickguard as standard, as well as a selection of custom colours. Three custom designed single coil pickups with individual polepieces housed in metal surrounds were selected via individual on/off switches located on the upper treble bout control plate, with further adjustment available on the control plate of the lower treble bout courtesy of master volume and master tone knobs positioned adjacent to the guitar's front-loading jack input.

With a one-piece bolt-on maple neck and a 7¼-inch radius, 21-fret rosewood fretboard, the VI's scale length measures 30 inches, between the Jazzmaster/Telecaster/Stratocaster scale length of 25½ inches and the Precision/Jazz Bass scale length of 34 inches. Ordinarily tuned to E-A-D-G-B-E (from low to high) and pitched an octave lower than a regular six-string guitar, the VI's unique tension and string gauges give it a very specific feel and sound that may be described as more focused and defined than a regular bass, while exhibiting significantly greater punch and power than a conventional guitar. It remains a compelling and distinctive sonic experience.

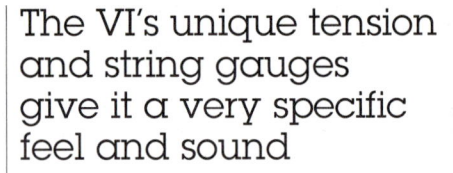

Danelectro's baritone guitar had hit the market back in 1956, so the six-string bass was already a studio favourite in Nashville, where producers famously made use of its muted 'tic-tac' sound. Innovation was still possible, however, and in 1963, following the release of the Fender Jaguar, the VI received a series of spec upgrades designed to accentuate this characteristic baritone sound, including a foam string mute, a fourth 'strangle'/bass-cut switch and 'sawtooth' Jaguar-style pickups.

Discontinued in 1975, the VI remains a unique piece of guitar history and although it was never a mainstream hit, it nonetheless managed to meet the distinguished approval of Jet Harris, Jack Bruce, John Entwhistle, John Lennon and George Harrison.

> **The VI's unique tension and string gauges give it a very specific feel and sound**

*Jaguar-style 'sawtooth' pickups replaced the model's original framed ones*

*This VI's 'Pink Champagne Sparkle' custom finish is a one-off*

*Individual switches engaged the VI's pickups*

## 1963 'Pink Champagne Sparkle' Fender VI

**1. SERIAL NUMBER**
L-prefixed five-digit serial number stamped onto metal neckplate

**2. HEADSTOCK**
Matching 'Pink Champagne Sparkle' finish; gold "Fender VI" logo with 'OFFSET Contour Body' decal

**3. PLASTICS**
'Mint green' celluloid pickguard; four black plastic switches; two black plastic knobs; foam string mute; ABS vinyl pickup covers

**4. HARDWARE**
Jazzmaster/Jaguar-style floating vibrato system; adjustable bridge with six individual saddles; 'Fender Mute' mechanism; two chrome control panels; single line Kluson tuners; single 'butterfly' string tree; two strap buttons; front-loading jack input

**5. PICKUPS**
Jaguar-style single coil pickups with individual pole pieces and notched metal sidepieces; individual on/off switches; 'strangle'/bass-cut switch; master volume and master tone pots

**6. BODY**
Offset Jazzmaster/Jaguar-style alder body with ultra-rare original 'Pink Champagne Sparkle' true custom colour finish

**7. NECK**
Single-piece bolt-on maple neck; 21-fret veneer rosewood fretboard with 'clay' dot inlays and 7¼-inch radius; 30-inch scale length

## The Evolution of the Fender VI

**1961**
VI released; slab rosewood fingerboard; three on/off pickup switches; metal pickup surrounds

**1963**
Foam string mute; 'strangle' switch added; notched metal Jaguar-style pickups; veneer 'board

**1964**
Plastic pickguard replaces celluloid type

**1965**
Bound fingerboard

**1966**
Block fingerboard inlays replace dots

**1968**
Black peghead logo replaces gold "Fender VI" logo; polyester replaces nitrocellulose finish

**1974**
Black pickguard introduced

**1975**
VI discontinued

**1995**
Fender MIJ reissue Bass VI released (discontinued 1997)

**2006**
Fender Custom Shop '64 Bass VI reissue released (discontinued 2008)

FEATURE | **Gibson & Fender Bass Guitars**

QUALITY MUSICAL INSTRUMENTS
★ *Original* ★
# HISTORIC HARDWARE
100% GUARANTEED
★★★

# ROYAL RUMBLE

Gibson's head of Product Development, Mat Koehler, and Fender historian Terry Foster explain how the two industry titans battled it out over the electric bass in the early days – and changed the course of popular music in the process...

**Words** Rod Brakes   **Photography** Olly Curtis, Neil Godwin & Jesse Wild

The post-war period of the early 50s was a time of great innovation. Following major advancements in instrument design after the war, radical developments at Fender saw the release of both the seminal Esquire and Broadcaster by 1950 (renamed the Telecaster in 1951). In 1952, Gibson's Les Paul Model similarly heralded the beginning of a new era in guitar building. As creativity flowed between musicians and guitar builders alike, popular culture and music technology moved forward in tandem and a new style of instrument began to take shape, beginning with Fender's Precision Bass in 1951, followed by the Gibson Electric Bass or EB-1 in 1953. As the decade progressed, the electric guitar industry's biggest rivals – Gibson in the east, Fender in the west – began battling it out for their stake in the expanding marketplace of electric basses.

"Commercially, Gibson was playing catch up with Fender from the start," begins Terry Foster, co-author of *Fender: The Golden Age 1946-1970*. "In 1950, the Broadcaster and Esquire came out, and in 1952 the Les Paul came out. It was the same thing when the Precision Bass came out in 1951 and then the EB-1 came out in 1953. That's a large expanse of time. And at that point there wasn't just the one almighty NAMM trade show twice a year; there were multiple trade shows all over the country. The Gibson representatives would have had a chance to check out those instruments multiple times and see the dealers' reactions. Then they'd go back and say, 'Okay, guys, we need something as well.'"

"The EB-1 was Gibson's first foray into electric bass and it was initiated by Fender's Precision Bass," confirms Mat Koehler, former proprietor of Santa Monica's Holy Grail Guitars and now head of Product Development at Gibson. "The reason they chose the violin shape with the leg extension was because of Les Paul's influence – the bassist in his trio played an upright bass. They were keenly aware of Fender, but [Gibson president] Ted McCarty didn't realise exactly what kind of a competition they were in. The EB-1 did not do well. It was not a commercial success. That's why Gibson later pursued the EB-2 and the EB-0 [released in 1958 and 1959 respectively].

"It's funny, I was just talking to my Epiphone cohorts here about how Ted

•

> *"You could argue that the Precision Bass had more of a cultural impact than anything else Fender did"*
> **TERRY FOSTER**

•

was still after Epiphone's upright basses in the late 50s, even when the Precision Bass was pretty standard across the music industry. He did want to counter that with the EB-1 early on, but he was still convinced upright basses were where it's at. The whole Epiphone thing started because Gibson were pursuing upright basses. The craziest story is that when Gibson purchased Epiphone [in 1957], Ted McCarty sent John Huis, his plant manager guy, to New York to evaluate what Epiphone had and oversee the transaction. They both thought they were purchasing Epiphone's upright bass business only, but when John went over there, he reported back to Ted, 'They think we're buying everything – the whole company!' We still have some of those original memos."

Although the Precision Bass was not the first fretted horizontal electric solidbody bass model on the market, having been preceded by Paul Tutmarc's pre-war era instruments, its design was a convincing move away from upright basses and marked a watershed in music history.

"Fender weren't the first to build an electric bass," concedes Terry. "There are some examples that existed before the P-Bass, but they're culturally irrelevant. The Tutmarcs were little short-scale things that didn't play very well, and it's unlikely that Leo Fender or anyone at the company ever saw one. Leo invented that [34-inch] scale length and virtually every [electric

*44* | LEGENDARY GUITARS

Released in 1951, the original incarnation of Fender's Precision Bass is reminiscent of a Telecaster with its narrow headstock and blonde/blackguard livery. This stunning example is from 1953

FEATURE | **Gibson & Fender Bass Guitars**

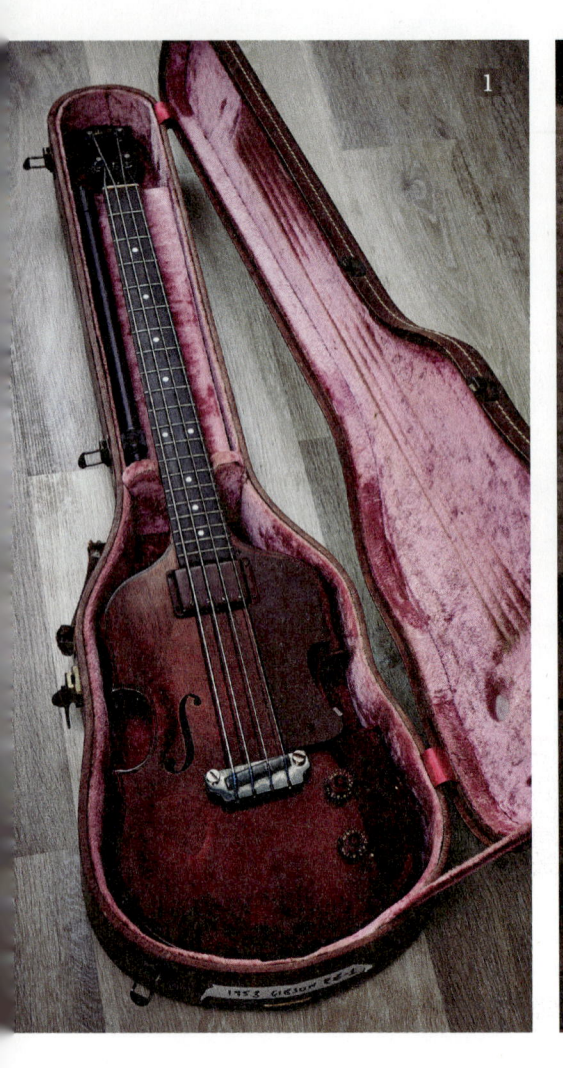

1. Gibson's Electric Bass was released in 1953 and came equipped with a detachable telescopic endpin for traditional upright players, as pictured in the case of this example from 1953

2. 1962 Fender Precision Bass: in 1959, Brazilian rosewood slab fretboards superseded fretted maple necks, and tortoiseshell celluloid pickguards were introduced as standard with Sunburst finishes

3. By 1957, with its redesigned headstock shape and the previous addition of rounded body contours, the Precision Bass had taken on a distinctly Strat-like appearance

bass] design that followed was derived from the Precision Bass. You could even argue that Leo inventing the Precision Bass had more of a cultural impact than anything else Fender did. It spanned virtually every genre of modern music. It would be hard for someone to argue against that.

"It's part of the soundtrack of the 20th century. In the early days when studios were calling for sessions, they asked for someone to either play 'bass', or the 'Fender bass', meaning the electric bass – the two things were synonymous."

"I'm a huge Leo Fender fan," remarks Mat. "And I think he nailed it on the very first try with the P-Bass. Even from Gibson's side I would argue that the Precision Bass is the most influential bass design ever. The fact that you didn't have to lug around an upright bass in your station wagon was a nice plus! It made the bass a lot more accessible for people. It just makes sense."

"It made perfect sense at the time," agrees Terry, "given what people were using for bass. It was the perfect solution to hauling around an enormous double bass, and it was a natural extension of the Fender line, especially once they had the ability to quickly scale things up. Don [Randall, Leo's business partner] was at the trade shows while Leo was in the clubs, and it would have struck them both as being an opportunity. People often think of Leo Fender as being nerdy and introverted, but he wasn't like that at all. He was great at talking to people and he enjoyed getting out there. Being passionate, patient and socially adept enough to have the right conversations with musicians was how a non-musician/designer like Leo navigated that information. Designing it is where the genius comes in."

Not only did the Precision Bass immediately look, sound and feel right to musicians, like so many enduring

> *"1958 is the red-letter year in Gibson's history… The ES guitars, Flying V, Explorer and the EB-2"*
> **MATT KOEHLER**

inventions of the modern era it also solved a few practical problems.

"The Precision Bass was an extremely practical answer to the double bass," says Terry. "First and foremost, the commercial success of the Precision Bass was due to solving the problems of portability, playability and precision. The name was suggested by Don and came about because it's fretted, as opposed to the fretless double bass. It's about precise fretting.

"It's easy to imagine that when the P-Bass arrived, a lot of people who were playing the double bass thought, 'Thank God!' I played the double bass in school and it's a pain in the ass. It's as tall as you are and as fat as two men! And you can't move around much on stage. It is a real struggle to play compared to the P-Bass. Plus you can't be heard easily, especially if the guitars have been amplified – and by that point in time they mostly would have been in one way or another. How do you take a Jaco Pastorius-style lead break in 1950 on one of those double basses? I mean, there were obviously guys who could play the shit out of those things, but once people had the tool that relieved all of those problems, things changed big-time.

46 | LEGENDARY GUITARS

**Gibson & Fender Bass Guitars** | FEATURE

**4.** Gibson's EB-2 was introduced at Chicago's NAMM show in July 1958 and was briefly discontinued in '61, before being reintroduced in '64; it was finally discontinued in the early 70s. This example is from 1966

**5.** This EB-2 headstock shows a pearl logo and crown inlays, nickel-plated tuners, a laminated plastic 'bell' truss rod cover, and a black nitrocellulose finish over a holly veneer

**6.** Appearing as early as 1960, the EB-2's bridge mute mechanism didn't prove to be a highly popular addition and was often rendered unusable as the rubber contact material perished

"The Precision Bass sparked a revolution. It changed everything. Suddenly, a bass player could be much nimbler. It was the same thing with the Telecaster: suddenly, guitarists had easy and full access to all the notes. It wasn't like it was before where you needed to be a genius bass player to play a complicated bass line. The tools change the rules of the game.

"Before the P-Bass arrived, a lot of bass players more or less played tuba lines, but that changed over time and you see a natural evolution in music from 1951, when the tool became available, to the way Paul McCartney played bass in The Beatles. And you don't have Paul without James Jamerson, right?"

Leo introduced several major alterations to the Precision Bass over the course of the decade, restlessly working to improve upon his original design.

"He was constantly tweaking the design," Terry points out. "No other Fender instrument changes so profoundly over the course of its lifespan during Don and Leo's tenure. They added the body contours in '54 when the Strat came out. Then [between '54 and '55] they changed the pickguard [from black to white] and the

LEGENDARY GUITARS | *47*

FEATURE | **Gibson & Fender Bass Guitars**

**7.** 1964 Epiphone Rivoli: essentially a rebranded version of the Gibson EB-2, Epiphone's Rivoli was introduced in 1959. It was constructed using the same methods and materials at Gibson's Kalamazoo factory

**8.** Aside from the Epiphone epsilon logo on the pickguard, the Rivoli can immediately be distinguished from the EB-2 by its headstock shape and inlays

Blonde finish to a Sunburst [as standard]. By 1957, it had changed to a [gold] anodised [aluminium] pickguard and the headstock shape changes, at which point it looks much more like a Stratocaster than a Telecaster. The new [split] humbucking pickup design [introduced in 1957] was a radical departure from the original, which was a variation of the Broadcaster pickup design."

Hot on Fender's heels shortly after the later incarnation of the Precision Bass arrived in 1957, Gibson struck back with the announcement of its new electric bass guitar design, the semi-hollowbody EB-2, at the now legendary July 1958 NAMM show in Chicago.

"1958 is the red-letter year in Gibson's history," highlights Mat. "I dream about that NAMM show and all the latest things that would've been there: ES guitars, the Flying V, the Explorer... And the EB-2 was a big part of the release as well. Ted McCarty said that in the shows before this, people were snickering that Gibson were still building old man's instruments – this was mainly coming from the West Coast camp. There was definitely a rift in design between the East Coast and the West Coast. The clean California designs in the mid-20th century were a pinnacle of modern minimalism and modernism, whereas Ted felt that Gibson needed to think outside of the box like the rest of the industry and move away from the old-school Michigan furniture building mentality.

"The EB-2 is arguably the greatest bass Gibson ever produced. Larry Allers was the man behind the design of both the EB-2 and the [solid-boded] EB-0. He was also responsible for designing the SG. The 'sidewinder' or 'mudbucker' humbucking pickup was designed by Walter Fuller, not Seth Lover, in Gibson's electronics division. In terms of number, the shipping figures show that the EB-0 was the most successful bass, but in terms of value as an instrument, I think the EB-2 has the longest enduring appeal and the same goes for the [Epiphone] Rivoli that appeared a year later, in '59; they're basically the same thing. The

•

*"Fender had feedback from the marketplace and was looking for something that worked for jazz players"*
**TERRY FOSTER**

•

Rivoli is such a cult classic. It actually sold much better than the EB-2."

Gibson's new basses had barely made a dent in the market when Fender promptly released its new and advanced follow-up to the Precision Bass in 1960, the Jazz Bass.

"The Jazz Bass mirrors the development of the Jazzmaster," explains Terry. "Fender had feedback coming from the marketplace and were looking for something that worked for jazz players. Some people find the J-Bass is easier to play because the strings are closer together, and Fender had the idea that the offset body worked better for people sitting down. Leo tweaked that design quite bit as well. The initial J-Bass pickups were essentially Jazzmaster pickups. And the Jazzmaster pickups come from the [model 1000 and 800 pedal] steel guitars. The first [prototype] design had three knobs, then it went to two concentric knobs, before going back to the original design [in 1962].

"But the change from maple to rosewood [across the Fender line from 1959] was not really the same sort of tweaking. That was feedback from the marketplace about the maple necks looking worn after a while. Fender thought people would just change the neck, but they totally miscalculated that one. Once the guitar's yours, it's yours,

**1964 Olympic White Fender Jazz Bass:** released in 1960 as an upscaled alternative to the P-Bass, the Jazz Bass features dual pickups and a slimmer neck profile

FEATURE | **Gibson & Fender Bass Guitars**

*1964 Gibson Thunderbird II: Gibson's Thunderbird II and IV electric basses were originally released in 'reverse' incarnation in 1963, and were later re-released with a 'non-reverse' design in 1965*

right? Especially when the neck shapes change so much over the years."

Anxious to cash in on the zeitgeist of the early 60s and boost its sales, Gibson decided to take a leaf from Fender's book and embrace the automotive industry's design aesthetics that were so popular with the upwardly mobile electric-guitar-buying youth of the day. The Thunderbird II and IV solid-bodied basses, released in 1963, embodied the angular geometry of classic car design and were suitably available in custom colours – a first for Gibson.

"I personally find the Thunderbird to be one of the coolest basses of all time," enthuses Mat. "Thunderbirds – and Firebirds – were created because Ted McCarty struck up a friendship with [retired car designer] Ray Dietrich, and the decision to use custom colours was because Fender were doing the same thing. I think the custom colour examples are very cool, but that reverse design was just too hard to

*"The reverse [Thunderbird] design was just too hard to produce [so] Gibson moved to non-reverse models"*
MATT KOEHLER

produce. It's much easier to create the non-reverse variety, and I believe that's mainly why Gibson moved to the non-reverse models [in 1965]. Gibson was able to price the non-reverse models lower and I think they sold much better because of that throughout the late 60s. There was a lot of interesting stuff happening in this industry at Fender and Gibson during that time, and I think some of it was just a direct response to the other."

"I think the Precision Bass was Leo Fender's crowning achievement," concludes Terry. "And his greatest post-Fender achievement is probably the Music Man StingRay bass [introduced in 1976]. You can even argue that had he stayed in charge at Fender, the P-Bass would have morphed into the StingRay bass, because he was constantly tweaking the design and, evidently, that's where he was headed. It seems the bass is what fascinated Leo the most. So the legend goes, the last thing he worked on at G&L – the day before he died – was a six-string bass." **G**

*Guitarist* would like to thank both Vintage 'n' Rare Guitars in Bath and ATB Guitars in Cheltenham

## FUNDAMENTAL SERIES

Introducing the Walrus Audio Fundamental Series. Designed with the tonal integrity that's required to live on a professional's pedalboard, but with simplified controls friendly enough for even the newest effect pedal users. Each Fundamental pedal has three sliders for sound tweaking and a three-way switch for changing pedal modes. The result is a line of pedals that will keep you covered from your first band practice to a sold-out arena.

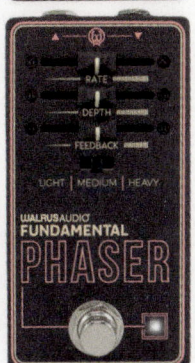

Learn more at walrusaudio.com

FACE Exclusive UK-Distribution - www.face.be

**DAZED & CONFUSED**

# GIBSON ELECTRIC ARCHTOPS

We shed light on some of the key differences between Gibson's early flagship models…

The first 'Electric Spanish' guitar produced by Gibson was the groundbreaking ES-150 in 1936. The company's solid/carved-top pre-war 'ES' range was gradually extended with the introduction of the ES-100 in 1938 (renamed the ES-125 by 1941) and the arrival of the short-lived ES-250 in 1939, along with its replacement, the ES-300, in 1940. Although World War II temporarily put the kibosh on electric guitar-building from 1942, Gibson soon returned to Electric Spanish production after the war with its revamped, laminated body designs, including the ES-125, ES-150 and ES-300 in 1946, followed by the single-cutaway ES-350P (Premier) in 1947.

In 1948 the ES-350P was upgraded with a dual-pickup assembly in tandem with the ES-300, whereupon it became known simply as the ES-350. At this point, it was clear that pickups were the future, and with Ted McCarty's arrival the same year Gibson's golden era of electric guitar design truly got underway with the triple P-90-loaded laminated body ES-5 appearing in 1949. With demand for electric guitars growing, equivalent versions of Gibson's foremost acoustics, the L-5 and Super 400, then followed. Thus, in 1951 the solid/carved-top L-5CES and Super 400CES (Cutaway Electric Spanish) became the firm's undisputed flagship archtops. **G**

## 1 ES-350

Essentially a 'Premier' (archaic Gibson speak for cutaway) version of its sibling, the ES-300, the ES-350 was introduced in 1947 as the ES-350P and enjoyed its moment in the sun as Gibson's primo electric archtop until the arrival of the ES-5 in 1949. With its gold-plated hardware, multiple pickups and single Venetian cutaway – a first for regular production Gibson electrics – it set a benchmark for future top-of-the-line models.

Like the ES-300, the ES-350 measures 17 inches across, has a full body depth of 3 3/8 inches and sports a 25½-inch scale length neck with a rosewood 'board inlaid with double-parallelogram markers. Its body is constructed using laminated maple and features unbound f-holes along with triple-binding on the top and back. A favourite of jazz stars Tal Farlow and Barney Kessel, it was phased out at the dawn of rock 'n' roll in 1956, having been superseded by the Chuck Berry-endorsed ES-350T (Thinline).

## 2 ES-5

When Gibson released the ES-5 in 1949 it was hailed as "the supreme electronic version of the famed Gibson L-5" – the Lloyd Loar-designed progenitor of all jazzboxes released earlier in 1923. But while the ES-5 borrowed its multiple-bound pointed fingerboard design and large pearl block inlays from the L-5, its body was more akin to the laminated-maple construction of the ES-350, with the same dimensions, single Venetian cutaway, triple-bound top and back, and unbound f-holes.

The ES-5 was originally loaded with three P-90 single coils that feature separate volume controls along with a master tone control, making it "the instrument of a thousand voices", according to Gibson. In 1955 it was dubbed the ES-5 Switchmaster while a four-way pickup selector switch was added and three separate tone controls replaced the single master tone knob. In 1957, the ES-5 was augmented with PAF humbuckers before eventually being discontinued by 1962.

## 3 L-5CES

Although Gibson initially claimed that the ES-5 was to be "the supreme electronic version" of the L-5, it was soon decided that a more faithful design was required in order to appeal to the upper echelons of the rapidly expanding electric guitar market. Subsequently, in 1951 the L-5CES was introduced, surpassing the ES-5 on all fronts as the L-5's electric sibling. More accurately, the L-5CES was derived from the single-cutaway L-5C (previously known as the L-5P or L-5 Premier).

The L-5CES may share the same body dimensions as the ES-5, but with its carved spruce top and solid maple back and sides its construction is fundamentally different. Furthermore, its fancy appointments and stylish ebony fretboard go on to place it in a different class to the plainer, rosewood-endowed ES-5 altogether.

The dual-pickup L-5CES was originally fitted with P-90s prior to the arrival of Alnico pickups in 1953. In 1958 these were supplanted by PAF humbuckers.

## 4 SUPER 400CES

With a design that originated from the 1934 Super 400 acoustic archtop, the Super 400CES was introduced in tandem with the L-5CES in 1951 and represented the pinnacle of Gibson's ingenuity and craftsmanship. Measuring 18 inches across and decked out with large fancy inlays, multiple-ply binding and gold-plated hardware from top to bottom, this model was the largest and dearest of Gibson's archtop family. Like all the aforementioned guitars, it was available in either Sunburst or Natural finishes as standard (the latter designated with an 'N' suffix).

With its carved spruce top and solid maple back and sides, the Super 400CES was similar in construction to the L-5CES and these two leading electrics followed the same trajectory with respect to pickup changes – moving from P-90s to Alnico units in late 1953, followed by PAFs in 1958 as standard. In 1960 the cutaway was changed to a Florentine design, before reverting to the original Venetian style in 1969.

LEGENDARY GUITARS

1 2
3 4

*Electric*Evolution

# Gibson ES-175

## With its Florentine cutaway, this hollowbody electric archtop was a Gibson first

Following its release in 1949, the 175 proved to be one of Gibson's most popular designs. Author Adrian Ingram calls it "Gibson's most successful electro-acoustic guitar" in his book *The Gibson ES175: Its History And Players*, quoting an estimated 37,000 having been sold within its first half-century of production alone. Like many classic guitars, the 175's essential layout didn't change a great deal after it came off the drawing board – its dynamic sound, comfy ergonomics and understated cool ticked all the right boxes from the start. This timeless design has consistently won guitar players over throughout the decades, and although it is perhaps more strongly associated with jazz virtuosos such as Joe Pass and Herb Ellis, it's just as likely to be spotted in the hands of rock guitarists like Steve Howe and John Frusciante.

The 175 came about during a turning point in Gibson's history. Having acquired the company in 1944, Chicago Musical Instruments' financial support aided Gibson in the pursuit of cutting-edge designs during the post-war years. Still, chairman of the board at CMI, Maurice Berlin, was concerned about the Kalamazoo factory's continued losses of "$100,000 per month". It would take a young engineering graduate turned music industry executive named Ted McCarty to turn things around.

Having resigned from Wurlitzer, Ted joined Gibson in 1948 and was immediately tasked with reversing its ailing fortunes by modernising the firm.

That year, Ted expanded Gibson's electric range with a pickup-loaded scratchplate design. Later known as the 'McCarty unit', this innovation came in either single- or dual-pickup formats for cutaway and non-cutaway guitars and led to the addition of several new electrified archtop models based on the L-7 acoustic. As per Gibson's pre-war electrics, however, these guitars were constructed with solid tops, backs and sides, and Ted's focus soon shifted to the newer laminate body 'ES' ("electric Spanish") line with the aim of developing a mid-priced cutaway model.

With a sunburst finish and costing $175 upon its release in 1949, the ES-175 had a Florentine/sharp cutaway, which was a Gibson first. Featuring double-parallelogram fretboard inlays along with a pearl Gibson logo and 'crown' headstock inlays, it was introduced alongside its acoustic equivalent, the L-4C. The ES-175

### Its dynamic sound, comfy ergonomics and understated cool ticked all the right boxes

has the same full 3 3/8-inch body depth that was standard for all other 'ES' guitars back then, though many players found its width of 16 1/4 inches to be more comfortable than the broader 17-inch-wide 'ES' guitars of the time, namely the ES-150, ES-300 and ES-350.

The original ES-175 is a single (neck) pickup guitar, although dual-pickup instruments were custom ordered in the early 50s on occasion. It wasn't until 1953 that the officially designated 'D'/dual pickup version – the ES-175D – was released. This followed the arrival of the $295 ES-295 in 1952 – a fancy all-gold finish guitar with dual pickups that was itself inspired by the ES-175 and marketed as the archtop companion to the 'Goldtop' Les Paul Model. While the ES-295 and ES-175 were discontinued in 1958 and 1971 respectively, the ES-175D went on to become one of the most enduring electric guitars ever designed by Gibson.

## The Evolution of the Gibson ES-175

**1949**
ES-175 released; single pickup; sunburst or natural finish

**1952**
ES-295 released; dual pickups; all-gold finish

**1953**
ES-175D released; dual pickups; sunburst or natural finish

**Mid-50s**
Some with 'alnico'/'staple' pickups (rare)

**1955**
20 frets (previously 19)

**1956**
Zig-zag 'T'-shaped tailpiece replaces pointed trapeze tailpiece

**1957**
PAF humbuckers replace P-90s

**1958**
ES-295 discontinued

**1959**
Natural-finish ES-175 discontinued

**1971**
Sunburst finish ES-175 discontinued

*Electric*Evolution

## 1959 Gibson ES-175D

**1. SERIAL NUMBER**
A-prefixed five-digit number ink-stamped onto orange oval label on rear of back (visible through bass f-hole)

**2. HEADSTOCK**
Unbound; pearl Gibson logo and crown inlays; black finish

**3. PLASTICS**
Two-ply (b/w) bell truss rod cover; white keystone tuner buttons; white pickup selector switch tip; black rubber switch grommet; five-ply (b/w/b/w/b) bevelled edge pickguard; two black pickup surrounds; four gold 'bonnet' knobs

**4. HARDWARE**
Nickel-plated zig-zag 'T'-shaped tailpiece; height-adjustable compensated rosewood bridge; individual Kluson Deluxe tuners

**5. PICKUPS & ELECTRONICS**
Two PAF humbuckers with independent volume and tone controls; three-way pickup selector switch; side-mounted jack socket

**6. BODY**
16 ¼ inches wide; 3 ⅜ inches deep; laminated maple with pressed, arched top; single Florentine cutaway; three-ply (w/b/w) top binding; single-bound back; two unbound f-holes; sunburst finish

**7. NECK**
Glued-in one-piece mahogany neck; 24 ¾-inch scale length; 14th-fret body join; single-bound 20-fret rosewood fingerboard with double-parallelogram inlays

*Guitarist* would like to thank Vintage 'n' Rare Guitars in Bath (www.vintageandrareguitars.com)

LEGENDARY GUITARS

*Electric*Evolution

# Gibson ES-125TDC

How Gibson's first budget electric archtop evolved (one letter at a time)…

The dual P-90 pickup single-cutaway ES-125TDC thinline electric archtop was manufactured at Gibson's Kalamazoo factory during the 1960s. In terms of features, it is the furthest evolved of the original ES-125 lineage – a family of electric archtops that has its roots in the pre-war era of the late 1930s when amplified guitars were just starting to become popular in the jazz world. The arrival of Gibson's 'Electric Spanish' (ES) range of archtops was heralded by the carved top ES-150 in 1936, and in 1938 the 'less expensive' alternative, the ES-100, became available. Sales proved successful and within a few years the ES-100 was renamed the ES-125, although by 1942 production had largely ceased following America's entry into World War II.

After the war, the demand for electric archtops was stronger than ever and Gibson soon recommenced production. By 1947, the company's new series of laminated body ES instruments included the revamped ES-125, ES-150 and ES-300, along with its Venetian cutaway sibling, the ES-350 Premier. These deep-bodied f-hole electric archtops all feature Gibson's post-war P-90 pickup and set the template for further laminated body designs. Partly due to its lower price point, the ES-125 was the most popular of the line and substantially outsold the other models, reaching its peak in 1953 with 3,713 instruments shipped.

This post-war period was a time of great innovation in electric-guitar design and musical styles were changing rapidly. With the advent of the solid-bodied electric guitar in the early 50s – notably Gibson's Les Paul range and Fender's Esquire, Telecaster and Stratocaster – the archtop's popularity began to wane, prompting Gibson to investigate new designs. Following suggestions from the marketplace, something of a compromise between the bulky feedback-prone archtops and the solid-bodied guitars appeared in 1955 with the introduction of three thinline electric archtops: the top-of-the-line carved top Byrdland (a combination of "popular recording and TV stars" Hank Garland and Billy Byrd's names) and the laminated body ES-350T and ES-225T guitars.

With its new thinlines proving an immediate success, Gibson wasted no time expanding the range and in 1956 released the ES-225TD, a dual P-90 single Florentine cutaway thinline similar in spec to the later ES-125TDC, and the ES-125T, a thinline version of the existing deep-bodied ES-125 electric archtop. In 1957, both the single-pickup ES-125T and ES-125 designs were augmented with an additional P-90

## With its new thinlines proving a success, Gibson wasted no time expanding the range

in the form of the ES-125TD and ES-125D respectively, while the Florentine cutaway ES-225T and ES-225TD models ran concurrently before being discontinued at the end of the 50s.

The ES-225T and ES-225TD were effectively replaced by the ES-125TC and ES-125TCD in 1960, and the following year the ES-125TCD was renamed the ES-125TDC. A promotional feature in the July/August 1960 edition of the *Gibson Gazette* reads, "Gibson announces a new Florentine cutaway style guitar! It's a new member of the ES-125 series… Comes equipped with either a single pickup (ES-125TC) or a double pickup (ES-125TCD). Gibson predicts a bright future for this finely crafted newest member of its line!"

Sales of both models were relatively strong throughout the decade, but dwindled considerably during the late 60s as popular musical styles further evolved. Ultimately, with Gibson under new ownership, the ES-125 range was eventually discontinued at the beginning of the 70s.

## The Evolution of the Gibson ES-125TDC

**1938**
ES-100 introduced (renamed ES-125 in 1941); deep-bodied electric archtop; single pickup

**1946**
ES-125 reintroduced; deep-bodied electric archtop; single P-90 pickup

**1955**
Thinline electric archtop designs introduced (Byrdland, ES-350T, ES-225T)

**1956**
ES-125T thinline non-cutaway electric archtop introduced; single P-90 pickup

**1957**
Non-cutaway ES-125TD thinline and deep-bodied ES-125D introduced; dual P-90s

**1959**
Single P-90 ES-225T and dual P-90 ES-225TD single-cutaway thinlines discontinued

**1960**
Single P-90 ES-125TC and dual P-90 ES-125TCD single-cutaway thinlines introduced

**1961**
ES-125TCD renamed ES-125TDC

**1965**
Chrome-plated tailpiece; deep-bodied ES-125C and ES-125CD introduced

**1970**
ES-125 range discontinued

*Electric*Evolution

### 1963 Gibson ES-125TDC

**1. SERIAL NUMBER**
Five digits impressed into upper rear of headstock

**2. HEADSTOCK**
Yellow silkscreen Gibson logo; black nitrocellulose finish

**3. HARDWARE**
Three-on-a-plate single-line Kluson Deluxe tuners; height-adjustable compensated rosewood bridge; nickel-plated trapeze tailpiece with raised diamond; adjustable truss rod

**4. NECK**
One-piece mahogany neck; 24¾-inches scale length; unbound 20-fret Brazilian rosewood fingerboard with pearl dot inlays; 14th-fret body join; nitrocellulose finish

**5. BODY**
Arched laminated maple top and back; laminated maple sides; single Florentine cutaway; 16¼ inches wide, 1¾ deep; single bound top and back; Cherry Sunburst nitrocellulose finish

**6. PLASTICS**
White tuner buttons; black 'bell' truss-rod cover; two black 'dog-ear' P-90 pickup covers; single-layer tortoiseshell pickguard; four metal cap bonnet knobs; white switch tip

**7. PICKUPS & ELECTRONICS**
Two 'dog-ear' P-90 pickups with adjustable polepieces; two tone capacitors; four CentraLab 500kohms pots (individual pickup volume and tone); three-way Switchcraft pickup selector toggle; side-mounted Switchcraft jack

*Guitarist* would like to thank Mike Long at ATB Guitars in Cheltenham (www.atbguitars.com)

LEGENDARY GUITARS | 57

*Electric*Evolution

# Gibson ES-330TD

Far from being a poor man's 335, the ES-330 is in a class of its own

In the mid 1950s, prior to the release of the ES-330TD in 1959, Gibson began to experiment with the form of their electric archtop designs by slimming down body depth. These guitars are often referred to as 'thinline' and in 1954 a trickle of L-5 'special thin models' appeared, followed in 1955 by the Byrdland, ES-350T and ES-225T models. Over the next couple of years, Gibson expanded its 'ES' (Electric Spanish), 'T' (Thinline) range to include the short scale ES-140¾T and the ES-125T. With dual pickup versions of the ES-125T and ES-225T becoming available soon thereafter, a 'D' was added to the model names accordingly. By 1959, however, both the ES-225T and ES-225TD guitars had

## The ES-330TD was less susceptible to feedback at high volume than full depth archtops

ceased production as Gibson introduced a new fully hollow double cutaway body design to the range: the $275 ES-330TD (along with its lesser known single pickup counterpart, the ES-330T).

The dual P-90 equipped ES-330TD thinline electric archtop arrived somewhat in the shadow of the dual humbucker toting ES-335TD, ES-345TD and ES-355TD electric semi-acoustics. Although comparisons were inevitable (perhaps superficially based on body shape, controls and finish), there are some major differences that set the ES-330TD a world apart from these guitars. Although perhaps less susceptible to feedback at high volume than a full depth electric archtop, the ES-330TD was notably more prone to unwanted noise than a guitar with pickups mounted into a solid centre block – especially one fitted with the newly introduced noise cancelling PAF humbucker pickups. The ever increasing popularity of high volume electric blues and rock 'n' roll prompted a more practical solution for guitarists pointing towards semi-acoustic and solidbody guitars and so the ES-330TD took a back seat.

Much like Gibson's semi-acoustic electrics of the time, the ES-330TD's body is constructed from laminated maple with a single bound, pressed arched top sporting two f-holes, along with a single bound back. The 24¾-inch scale glued in mahogany neck joins the body lower down the bound rosewood fretboard than the ES-335/345/355TD guitars (up until 1968) and along with a fully hollow body and trapeze tailpiece this further sets it apart in terms of unplugged natural acoustics, with a deeper, rounder and louder tone.

The P-90 pickups, being relatively assertive in character with a fairly sharp attack and high output, effectively balance the sound with a pronounced midrange and tasteful grittiness, especially when driving the front end of the amplifier. There's some fun to be had when pushing the volume up into the edge of feedback, which can produce some interesting tonal effects with blooming overtones and dynamic sustain.

The design of the Gibson ES-330TD was, more or less, replicated at Gibson's Kalamazoo factory as part of the Epiphone brand range in the form of the Casino, released in 1961. Although it gained a great deal more publicity than the ES-330TD as a preferred guitar of The Beatles, there was little difference with regards to basic design features between the two instruments. **G**

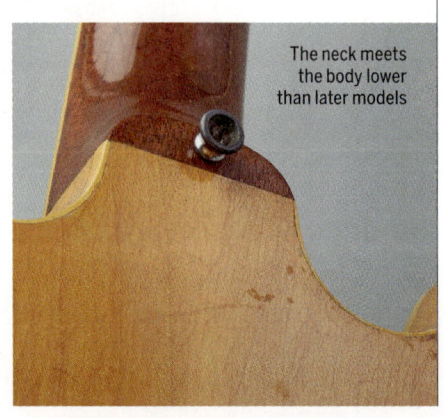

## The Evolution of the Gibson ES-330TD

**1959**
Released in Sunburst and Natural finishes; dot inlays; black plastic pickup covers

**1961**
Serial numbers appear on back of peghead in place of/in addition to FONs

**1962**
Cherry finish available; block inlays; rounded 'Micky Mouse ears' become slimmer

**1963**
Nickel pickup covers now standard

**1965**
Chrome plated hardware and pickup covers; narrower nut width introduced

**1967**
Sparkling Burgundy finish available

**1968**
Neck/body join moves from 16th to 19th fret (referred to as 'long necks'); Walnut finish available

**1969**
Sparkling Burgundy finish discontinued

**1972**
Discontinued

*Upping the volume can deliver some gritty tones*

*The neck meets the body lower than later models*

## 1959 Gibson ES-330TDN (Natural)

**1. SERIAL NUMBER**
No serial number; S-prefixed FON (Factory Order Number) only ink stamped onto back

**2. HEADSTOCK**
Gold 'modernised' script logo; no peghead ornamentation/inlays

**3. PLASTICS**
Four-ply black/white/black/white pickguard; two-ply black/white 'bell' truss rod cover; two black P-90 pickup covers; four clear, gold backed, flared base bonnet knobs

**4. HARDWARE**
Nickel plated, raised diamond trapeze tailpiece; nickel plated adjustable tune-o-matic bridge with metal saddles set into top/braces; three-a-side Kluson Deluxe tuners with white plastic buttons

**5. PICKUPS**
Two high output single-coil P-90 pickups with adjustable pole pieces; three-way pickup selector switch; four pots (two independent volume and tone controls)

**6. BODY**
16-inch wide, fully hollow double cutaway thinline; laminated maple top, back and sides with pressed arched top; single top and back binding; rare natural/'blonde' finish

**7. NECK**
24¾-inch scale glued in one piece mahogany joining the body at the 16th fret; single-bound Brazilian rosewood fretboard with 22 jumbo frets

*Electric*Evolution

# Gibson ES-335TD

The archtop that presented the best of the solidbody and acoustic worlds

In 1958, with jazz and the blues fully amped up, Gibson debuted the ES-335TD as the original 'Thinline' 'Double-pickup', double-cutaway, semi-acoustic archtop. It was a logical conclusion to the rich history of Gibson's 'ES' (Electric Spanish) lineage that began in 1936 with the Charlie Christian-endorsed ES-150. Over the next couple of decades, Gibson worked towards something of an apex with the ES-335TD via a series of profound design concepts. In 1949, the ES-175 was introduced with a single cutaway, gaining double pickups in 1953 as the ES-175D. In 1954, the Byrdland (a portmanteau of the names Billy Byrd and Hank Garland), which was in its early incarnation documented as the L-5 Special Thin Model, profiled a reduced body depth. This was shortly followed by the ES-350T in 1955 (later renamed ES-350TD), which also featured a reduced body depth, cutaway and double pickups.

As an addition to a well-established line of f-hole archtops, the ES-335TD broke further ground with its double cutaway and semi-acoustic/centre-block features, augmented by Gibson's new and improved noise-cancelling 'humbucking' pickups. Along with increased access to the upper frets enabling guitarists to easily hit notes and bend strings high up the neck, its solid maple centre-block snugly housed and surrounded both pickups, firmly suppressing the feedback that had plagued archtop players for years. The ES-335TD thus employed the solidbody signature-feature of recessing pickups into a small cavity (a tried and tested method since Gibson released the Les Paul in 1952), while enjoying some of the natural acoustic resonance of a traditional archtop. Part solidbody/part acoustic, the innovative 'semi-acoustic' hybrid guitar successfully balanced the best of both worlds.

## Cherry On The Top

The original ES-335TD released in 1958 sported a one-piece glued mahogany neck with a Brazilian rosewood 'board and dot inlays, joining the body at the 19th fret. The body measured 16 inches across and consisted of an arched, single-bound laminated maple top and back. It was mounted with a tune-o-matic bridge and stop tailpiece (Bigsby optional) and finished in either Sunburst or Natural (ES-335TDN). The iconic Cherry finish (ES-335TDC) was offered later in 1959. Some design adjustments were subsequently made throughout its production, although it hasn't altered radically since its introduction, with reissues catering for notable preferences in specification, without needing to invest in the highly collectible original vintage models. (Interestingly, the ES-335 is worth considerably more on the vintage market than equivalent-year ES-345 and/or ES-355, although both of these models were pricier than the ES-335 upon original release.)

Along with the ES-335TD's ability to push the envelope in terms of gain and a warm, plangent fullness of tone, it struck a very happy medium between feedback and sustain, endowing players with a flexible and colourful palette of sounds at their fingertips. It was famously embraced by blues players and as a particularly dynamic instrument has also enjoyed popularity within a diverse range of guitar styles since its arrival, with ES-335 signature models having been produced by Gibson in association with artists as diverse as Trini Lopez, Eric Clapton, Larry Carlton, Chris Cornell, Lee Ritenour, Roy Orbison, Tom DeLonge, Alvin Lee ("Big Red" ES-335), Andy Summers (1960 ES-335) and Dave Grohl (DG-335). With an expressive, vocal characteristic, the ES-335TD's continued popularity and longevity since its introduction in 1958 speaks in volumes.

## The Evolution Of The Gibson ES-335TD

**1957**
ES-335TD developed

**1958**
Gibson ES-335TD launched (originally as ES-335T); official production begins in spring

**1959**
Iconic Cherry finish available in addition to Sunburst and Natural

**1960**
Neck profile becomes less chunky; thinner/flatter 'blade' necks appear

**1961**
Shorter pickguard transition complete

**1962**
Pearloid blocks replace dot inlays

**1964**
Transition begins towards trapeze tailpiece; stop tailpieces becoming less common

**1965**
Nickel plated hardware replaced by chrome hardware; nut decreases in width

**1966**
Brazilian rosewood fretboard replaced by Indian rosewood

*Electric*Evolution

## 1961 Gibson ES-335TD

### 1. SERIAL NUMBER
'A'-prefixed five-digit number inked on orange oval soundhole label

### 2. HEADSTOCK
Mother-of-pearl Gibson logo and crown inlays; black finish

### 3. PLASTICS
Multiple-ply short pickguard (doesn't extend below the bridge); b/w 'bell' truss rod cover; white 'keystone' tuner buttons; black pickup surrounds; white switch tip; four 'bonnet' knobs (two volume and two tone)

### 4. HARDWARE
Nickel-plated: Kluson Deluxe tuners; pickup covers; tune-o-matic bridge; stop tailpiece

### 5. PICKUPS
Two PAF humbuckers; four pots (independent tone and volume); two tone capacitors; three-way selector switch; front-mounted jack

### 6. BODY
16 inches wide; 1 ¾ inches deep; laminated maple; maple centreblock; rounded double-cutaway; bound top and back; two unbound f-holes; cherry nitrocellulose finish

### 7. NECK
Mahogany; 24 ¾-inch scale; bound, 22-fret Brazilian rosewood fretboard with dot inlays; 19th-fret body join

LEGENDARY GUITARS | 61

*Electric*Evolution

# Gibson Les Paul Standard

The guitar that launched a thousand heroes

In the mid-1940s, famed guitarist Les Paul began work on his new invention: a radical solidbody electric guitar design nicknamed 'The Log'. Although his brainchild was initially rejected by Gibson, it was through enduring self-belief (not to mention the successful release of Fender's solidbody Telecaster forerunners, the Esquire and Broadcaster) that Les was eventually welcomed into the Gibson fold as a consultant in 1950. In 1951, company president Ted McCarty, along with factory manager John Huis, further researched, developed and eventually prototyped this revolutionary guitar with Les, concluding in the release of Gibson's first solidbody electric, the Les Paul Model, in 1952.

During the illustrious 'golden era' of Gibson guitar production in the 1950s, Les Paul Models were, fittingly, finished in gold to begin with and are therefore commonly referred to as 'Goldtops' (aside from a few ultra-rare exceptions). In 1952, the Les Paul Model – renamed the Les Paul Standard in 1958 – was fitted with two single-coil P-90 pickups and is easily distinguished by its trapeze 'strings under the bar' bridge/tailpiece, which was swiftly replaced in 1953 by a 'wrapover' stud bridge/tailpiece, allowing players to palm-mute strings.

Several more technical improvements were to follow: the neck angle was deepened in 1954, giving better all-round playability and sustain, and in 1955 the 'wrapover' bridge was in turn replaced with the intonation-friendly Tune-o-matic bridge and 'stop' tailpiece.

Perhaps the greatest technical leap forward, however, came in 1957 with the introduction of the humbucking pickup. Designed with noise cancellation in mind, the PAF humbucker (named after the 'Patent Applied For' sticker on the bottom of the early pickups) really gave the Les Paul Standard its pre-eminent tone and would make it a firm favourite in the hands of future guitar heroes.

## Burst Of Colour

In 1958, the Gibson Les Paul Standard was given a makeover and the gold finish was replaced with a classic Cherry Red Sunburst over a two-piece bookmatched maple top; these guitars are now known colloquially as 'Bursts. Although deemed a failure at the time by Gibson due to poor sales, the 'Bursts are often considered among today's players and collectors to be some of the most desirable electric guitars ever made, with prices well into six figures due to their relative scarcity (according to shipping records there were just over 1,700 Les Paul Standards produced from 1958 to 1960, though not all were 'Bursts).

By the end of 1960, the body design was radically overhauled into the double-cutaway SG shape, with Les's name eventually being removed altogether by 1963. It wasn't until 1968 that the original single-cutaway Les Paul body shape was to re-emerge from the Gibson factory due to a surge in demand, as the guitar was popularised by notable players such as Eric Clapton, Keith Richards and Peter Green during the 60s. Since then, it has been seen in the hands of countless guitarists across various genres, and to this day the Les Paul Standard endures as arguably Gibson's most iconic solidbody electric guitar of all time. G

> It wasn't until 1968 that the original single-cutaway Les Paul body shape re-emerged from the Gibson factory

## The Evolution of the Les Paul Standard

**1952**
Introduced as the Les Paul Model with two single-coil P-90 pickups

**1953**
'Wrapover' stud bridge/tailpiece replaces trapeze bridge/tailpiece; serial number appears on headstock

**1954**
Shallow neck angle deepened for improved action and sustain

**1955**
Tune-o-matic bridge and stop tailpiece added

**1957**
PAF humbuckers added

**1958**
Renamed 'Les Paul Standard'; two-piece maple top with Cherry Red Sunburst finish

**1959**
Larger frets introduced; neck profile less chunky than previous year

**1960**
Slim neck profile; changes to SG body shape at end of year

**1968**
Single-cut Les Paul Standard body shape reintroduced and production continues up to present

## 1960 Gibson Les Paul Standard

### 1. SERIAL NUMBER
Inked in black on headstock upper rear in 'x xxxx' configuration (first digit denoting year)

### 2. HEADSTOCK
Mother-of-pearl Gibson logo; gold decal reads 'Les Paul Model' black finish

### 3. PLASTICS
White pickguard; white pickup surrounds; gold 'bonnet' knobs; white switch tip; white switch ring (labelled 'rhythm' and 'treble'); white 'keystone' tuner buttons; b/w 'bell' truss rod cover; white jack plate

### 4. HARDWARE
Nickel-plated: Kluson Deluxe tuners; pickup covers; tune-o-matic bridge; stop tailpiece

### 5. PICKUPS
Two PAF humbuckers; four pots (independent tone and volume); two tone capacitors; three-way selector switch; side-mounted jack

### 6. BODY
1 ¾ inches deep; solid mahogany; arched two-piece figured maple top; single-cutaway; bound top; cherry red sunburst nitrocellulose finish (faded)

### 7. NECK
Mahogany; 24 ¾-inch scale; bound, 22-fret Brazilian rosewood fretboard with trapezoid inlays; 16th-fret body join

*Guitarist* would like to thank Andrew Raymond of Vintage 'n' Rare Guitars in Bath

*Electric*Evolution

# Late-60s Gibson Les Paul Custom

Back by popular demand, the 'black beauty' returns ready to rock

Gibson's debut solidbody guitar line was introduced in 1952 with the Les Paul Model (dubbed the 'Goldtop' on account of its gold finish). The range was expanded in 1954 with the Les Paul TV and Junior student guitars along with the price-list-topping Ebony finish Les Paul Custom. The mid-priced Les Paul Special was added the following year. At this stage, Les Paul Customs featured an Alnico V pickup in the neck position paired with a P-90 in the bridge position, while all other Les Paul guitars were fitted with P-90s only. From 1957, Customs were fitted with a trio of PAF humbuckers (rarely two), while the Goldtop received a dual set. The next year, the Les Paul Model was renamed the Les Paul Standard and decked out in its now iconic Cherry Sunburst finish. But the Standard would only be in production from 1958 to 1960 when it was radically overhauled into the SG-style double-cutaway design. Customs followed suit in 1961, appearing in a white finish yet retaining their triple-humbucker configuration.

The demise of the single-cutaway Les Pauls in the early 60s was attributed to poor sales. Furthermore, from the late 50s Gibson placed great emphasis on electric guitar designs that improved access to the upper frets, as evidenced by its modernised 1958 unveilings that included the ES-335, EB-2, Explorer, Flying V and double-cutaway TV and Junior Les Pauls. Advertised as a "new, revolutionary body design", the "fretless wonder" Les Paul Custom was renamed the SG Custom in 1963. SG (solid guitar) models generally sold well. But at the same time, a demand for the old-style Les Pauls was growing. Seen in the hands of guitar heroes from the mid-60s onwards, single-cutaway models were increasingly sought out by players and Gibson took note.

In 1968, Gibson reintroduced the single-cutaway Les Paul design in two guises: the Les Paul Standard and Les Paul Custom. With its gold finish and P-90 pickups, this Les Paul Standard differed considerably from its 'Burst namesake model that was in production from 1958 to 1960 and was supplanted by the mini-humbucker-loaded Les Paul Deluxe in 1969. The Deluxe became

## Gibson shipped more Les Paul Custom models in 1969 alone than it did throughout the entire 50s

a classic in its own right during the hard-rock era of the 70s but was discontinued in the mid-80s. Additionally in '69, with Les Paul himself now back onboard, Gibson expanded the single-cutaway line to include the short-lived Professional and Personal guitars (superseded by the Recording model in 1971). However, the most successful of all was the Custom. In fact, Gibson shipped more in '69 alone than it did throughout the entire 50s.

Though Gibson touted the late-60s Les Paul Custom as an "exact duplicate of the original", it differs significantly from the 50s guitars. The most obvious difference is that it came fitted with two humbuckers as standard. But less apparent is that underneath its Ebony finish lies a maple cap (earlier variants were constructed of mahogany only). Another important distinction is the headstock angle, which by this stage had been decreased from 17 to 14 degrees. Unique in construction, late-60s Les Pauls are coveted by collectors and are now commanding five-figure sums on the vintage market. G

## The Evolution of the Late-60s Les Paul Custom

**1952**
Les Paul Model released; single-cutaway body; 2x P-90 pickups; gold finish

**Late 1953**
Les Paul Custom prototypes

**1954**
Les Paul Custom released; single-cutaway; 1-piece mahogany body; Alnico V (neck) and P-90 (bridge) pickups; black finish

**1957**
3x humbuckers

**1961**
Double-cutaway SG-style mahogany body; 3x humbuckers; white finish

**1968**
Single-cutaway; 1-piece mahogany body with maple top; 1-piece mahogany neck; 2x humbuckers; black finish

**1969**
3-piece mahogany neck; shorter neck tenon

**Late 1969/Early 1970 (Norlin era)**
Laminated 'pancake' body with maple top; neck volute

**1972**
Les Paul Custom '54; Alnico V (neck) & P-90 (bridge) pickups; black finish

**1974**
'Twentieth anniversary' 15th fret inlay

Gold-plated hardware features throughout, including the Tune-o-matic bridge, tailpiece, pickup covers and tuners

*Electric*Evolution

## 1969 Gibson Les Paul Custom

**1. SERIAL NUMBER**
Six digits located on upper headstock rear

**2. HEADSTOCK**
Mother-of-pearl Gibson logo and five-piece split-diamond inlays; five-ply (b/w) binding; Ebony finish

**3. PLASTICS**
Two black pickup surrounds; multiple-ply (b/w) bevelled-edge pickguard; four black 'witch hat' knobs (two 'vol' and two 'tone') with gold labels; white switch tip; black switch ring (labelled 'rhythm' and 'treble'); two-ply (b/w) 'bell' truss rod cover (labelled 'Les Paul Custom'); black control cavity cover

**4. HARDWARE**
Gold-plated: two pickup covers, six 'waffle' tuners with metal buttons, Tune-o-matic bridge and stop tailpiece; metal strap buttons

**5. PICKUPS & ELECTRONICS**
Dual humbuckers; four pots (two volume, two tone); two tone capacitors; three-way selector switch; side-mounted jack

**6. BODY**
Single-piece mahogany; arched maple top; single-cutaway; seven-ply top binding; five-ply back binding; Ebony finish

**7. NECK**
Single-piece mahogany; long tenon; 24 ¾-inch scale length; 16th-fret body join; bound ebony fretboard with large mother-of-pearl block inlays; 22 low frets; Ebony finish

*Guitarist* would like to thank Seven Decades for showing us this incredible example

LEGENDARY GUITARS | 65

*Electric*Evolution

# Gibson Les Paul/SG Standard

This classic-rock machine has been a mainstay of Gibson's catalogue

Gibson's debut solidbody line got off to a great start following the release of the Les Paul Model/Goldtop in 1952. By 1957, however, Les Paul sales had tailed off significantly. Facing stiff competition from Fender, company president Ted McCarty and his design team doubled down on their efforts to come up with exciting, innovative products. Diving deep for new ideas, Gibson surfaced with a plethora of now iconic designs in 1958. Among them were the Explorer, Flying V, ES-335 and electric double-neck guitars (the Double 12 and Double Mandolin). Also that year, the Goldtop was revamped with a sunburst finish and renamed the Les Paul Standard. Meanwhile, the single-P-90 Les Paul Junior and TV guitars changed from single- to double-cutaway bodies.

Easy access to the upper frets was a major selling point, as evidenced on all of Gibson's new designs. The company deemed its double-cutaway Les Pauls to be "ultra-modernistic in appearance and practical in performance", and the dual P-90 Les Paul Special followed suit in 1959. That year, it was renamed the SG Special (SG stands for Solid Guitar) and appeared alongside the similarly rebranded SG TV. These solidbodies were the first to receive the 'SG' designation, but with their rounded double-cutaways and slab bodies they appear markedly different to the archetypal Gibson SG profile that came shortly afterwards.

Consistently poor sales of the flagship Les Paul Standard and Custom models throughout the late 50s and into 1960 prompted Gibson to cease production of the debut single-cutaway style and return to the drawing board. Although the original Les Paul blueprint would make a return in 1968 due to demand following endorsement by the likes of Keith Richards, Eric Clapton and Jeff Beck, what Gibson wanted back in 1960 was a brand-new design – something that would make an impact and claw back the company's success within a rapidly expanding solidbody market.

The first of Gibson's "new" Les Paul Standards were shipped towards the end of 1960 and were followed by the "completely redesigned" Les Paul Customs in early 1961. They appeared alongside each other in promotional literature that read, "thinner, lighter in weight and custom contoured… Combination bridge and tailpiece is a Gibson first – can be moved up or down to adjust tension." This Gibson 'sideways' Vibrola divides opinion, and many players prefer an SG sans vibrato system. Nevertheless, the firm persisted with the idea, later fitting several types including the 'leaf & lyre' Maestro Vibrola, the 'short' Vibrola (with or without a pearl-inlaid ebony block) and the Bigsby B-5 model.

## Easy access to the upper frets was a major selling point on all of Gibson's new designs

In 1961, the remaining Les Paul models adopted the new thin, contoured, pointed double-cutaway solid mahogany body styling. Thus, before the year was out, the full-size line-up comprised the Cherry Les Paul Standard and Les Paul Junior, and White Les Paul Custom, SG Special and SG TV (the Special was also available in Cherry). In 1963, Les Paul's name was dropped from the Custom, Standard and Junior guitars as the entire solidbody range was designated SG.

Officially known as the SG Standard from '63, this classic guitar has been famously played by some of the biggest names in rock including Eric Clapton, George Harrison and Angus Young.

'Short' and 'sideways' Vibrolas along with Bigsby B5s were fitted prior to the 'leaf and lyre' Maestro Vibrola becoming standard in 1963

## The Evolution of the Gibson Les Paul/ SG Standard

### 1958
Rounded double-cutaway Les Paul Junior & TV; Les Paul Model renamed Standard

### 1959
Rounded double-cutaway Les Paul Special; Les Paul TV & Special renamed SG

### 1960
Pointed double-cutaway Les Paul Standard supersedes single-cutaway design

### 1961
Pointed double-cutaway Les Paul Junior & Custom and SG TV & Special

### 1963
Les Paul Standard, Junior and Custom renamed SG

### 1965
Nickel-plated hardware switches to chrome; nut narrows from 1 11/16" to 1 9/16" or 1 5/8"

### 1966
Large 'bat-wing' pickguard (no pickup surrounds)

### 1971
Superseded by SG Deluxe; semi-circular control plate; small block markers

### 1972
SG Standard reintroduced; 'harmonica' bridge; small block markers

### Mid-1980s
SG-62 (first Les Paul/ SG Standard reissue)

*Electric*Evolution

## 1962 Gibson Les Paul/ SG Standard

**1. SERIAL NUMBER**
Five digits on headstock rear

**2. HEADSTOCK**
Mother-of-pearl Gibson logo and 'crown' inlays; black nitrocellulose finish

**3. BODY**
Mahogany; 1 5/16-inch depth; contoured edges; pointed double-cutaway; Cherry nitrocellulose finish

**4. PLASTICS**
Black pickup surrounds; black pickup/neck spacer; multi-ply (b/w) bevelled edge pickguard; four 'reflector' knobs (two volume/two tone); white switch tip; black switch ring (reads 'rhythm/ treble'); white keystone tuner buttons; black/ white 'bell' truss rod cover (reads 'Les Paul')

**5. HARDWARE**
Nickel-plated: pickup covers, Kluson Deluxe tuners, Tune-o-matic bridge and 'short' Vibrola; pearl-inlaid ebony block; two metal strap buttons

**6. PICKUPS & ELECTRONICS**
Dual humbuckers; two pots (two volume/two tone); two tone capacitors; three-way pickup selector; front-mounted jack

**7. NECK**
Mahogany; joins body at 22nd fret; 22-fret bound Brazilian rosewood fingerboard with pearloid trapezoid markers; 24 3/4-inch scale length; 1 11/16-inch nut width; Cherry nitrocellulose finish

*Guitarist* would like to thank Vintage 'n' Rare Guitars in Bath for showing us this 1962 Gibson Les Paul Standard

LEGENDARY GUITARS | 67

*Electric*Evolution

# Gibson Melody Makers

Gibson's "greatest value ever" electric solidbodies appeared in an array of designs

At first glance, the 1959 debut Melody Maker closely resembles the original single-cut, sunburst-finish Les Paul Junior introduced earlier in 1954. Similarly constructed using a mahogany slab-body and neck with an unbound 22-fret Brazilian rosewood 'board featuring dot markers, it's clear where this single-pickup guitar takes its design cues from. But with a depth of just 1 3/8-inch, the body of the Melody Maker is significantly thinner than the 1 3/4-inch deep Junior. Its headstock, too, is more slender than the Junior's. With a straighter appearance it forgoes Gibson's iconic profile.

> It's the PU-380 pickup that really sets the Melody Maker apart from the Les Paul Junior in terms of sound

However, it's the PU-380 pickup that really sets the Melody Maker apart in terms of sound. (For a great demo, check out Chris Buck's *Friday Fretworks* YouTube episode 'A 60s Gibson for less than a new one?!') Inherited from Gibson's Skylark lap steel, this single-coil unit was simply built by winding 42-gauge wire around an Alnico bar magnet for roughly 8,500 turns to give a DC resistance reading around 7kohms. It's a similar concept to the archetypal Fender pickup, the obvious difference being the PU-380 does not feature separate polepieces. It was initially constructed with a grey fibre bobbin, before a moulded nylon type was introduced in 1960. For this reason, older Melody Makers have slightly wider pickup covers. PU-380s can also be spotted on Gibson's ES-120T electric archtop, as well as the Epiphone-brand equivalents of the Melody Makers, the Olympics.

Similar to a Strat (or indeed Gibson's 'McCarty unit' of the late 1940s), the Melody Makers' pickups and electronics are attached to the instrument's pickguard. In the case of the debut Melody Maker and its shorter 22 3/4-inch-scale Melody Maker 3/4 sibling, this amounts to a single PU-380 positioned near the bridge, plus volume and tone controls. Meanwhile, the Melody Maker D/Double (listed in late '59 and first shipped the following year) sports an additional PU-380 at the neck, independent volume and tone controls for each pickup, and a three-way selector switch.

In 1961, the Melody Makers changed from a single- to double-cutaway design, and in 1965 the body shape altered yet again to incorporate pointier horns spaced slightly further apart, while the neck join moved from the 16th to the 18th fret. At this point, the standard finish switched from sunburst to cherry red. Full access to the upper frets was high on Gibson's agenda, and in 1966 the Melody Maker line followed in the footsteps of the Les Paul range by converting to the iconic SG style, whereupon a choice of two regular finishes were introduced: Pelham Blue and Fire Engine Red. At the same time, the pickguard and pickup covers changed from black to white and a vibrato unit became standard.

The following year, Gibson introduced triple-pickup and 12-string versions, the Melody Maker III and Melody Maker-12. Nevertheless, come the early 70s, all five SG-style Melody Makers were dropped from the catalogue. The Melody Maker and Melody Maker Double were effectively replaced by the short-lived SG 100/100-W and SG 250/200/200-W, respectively.

*According to Gibson's 1960 catalogue, the Melody Maker is "acclaimed by players, teachers and students for its fine sound, big tone [and] sensitive pickup"*

## The Evolution of the Gibson Melody Maker

**Early 1959**
Melody Maker & Melody Maker 3/4 introduced; single-cutaway; 1x pickup

**Late 1959**
Melody Maker D introduced; single-cutaway; 2x pickups

**1960**
Pickup cover narrows from 7/8" to 5/8"

**1961**
Double-cutaway; 16th-fret neck/body join retained; compensated 'lightning' bar bridge/tailpiece

**1962**
Vibrato optional

**1965**
Sharper double-cutaway horns; 18th-fret neck/body join; cherry red replaces sunburst finish

**1966**
SG-style body; Pelham Blue or Fire Engine Red finishes; vibrato standard

**1967**
Melody Maker III (3x pickups) & Melody Maker-12 introduced; Pelham Blue or Sparkling Burgundy finishes

**1969**
Walnut finish (exc. Melody Maker-12); Melody Maker 3/4 discontinued

**1971**
All discontinued; replaced by SG 100/100-W (MM) & SG 250/200/200-W (MMD)

*Electric*Evolution

## 1963 Gibson Melody Maker D

**1. SERIAL NUMBER**
Six digits on upper rear of headstock

**2. HEADSTOCK**
Narrow profile; gold Gibson logo decal; black nitrocellulose finish

**3. PLASTICS**
White oval tuner buttons; black truss rod cover; single-ply black pickguard embossed 'Melody Maker'; two black pickup covers; four 'reflector' knobs; white switch tip

**4. HARDWARE**
Nickel-plated: compensated bridge (Maestro Vibrola removed) and open-back strip tuners

**5. PICKUPS**
Attached to pickguard: two PU-380 single coils with independent volume and tone controls (four pots); three-way selector switch; jack

**6. BODY**
Solid mahogany; 1 3/8-inch deep; symmetrical double-cutaway; sunburst nitrocellulose finish

**7. NECK**
Mahogany; 24 3/4-inch scale; unbound, 22-fret Brazilian rosewood fingerboard with dot markers; joins body at 16th fret

*Guitarist* would like to thank Brandy Row for showing us this fantastic example

PHOTO BY OLLY CURTIS

LEGENDARY GUITARS | 69

**DAZED & CONFUSED**

# REVERSE GIBSON FIREBIRDS

With eight designs, four models and two body shapes, Gibson's Firebirds were anything but one and the same…

There have been numerous Firebird reincarnations since they were discontinued in 1970, but during their original run at Gibson's Kalamazoo factory in the 60s, the Firebird I, III, V and VII models appeared in two different forms widely known as 'reverse' and 'non-reverse'. The Explorer-like reverse Firebirds appeared first in 1963 and were superseded by their non-reverse counterparts in 1965.

As if eight different Firebirds emerging within this short time isn't convoluted enough, the waters muddy even further with some instruments having left the factory during the 1965 transition phase with both reverse and non-reverse specs. Nevertheless, here we aim to clear things up and make it simple for you to identify all four of the early reverse-style Firebird models at a glance.

Announced in the spring of '63, they were intended to compete directly with Fender and boost Gibson's flagging solidbody sales. However, Fender argued the Firebirds' "new style offset body" mirrored its own patented "off-set waist" body shape and, following talks, Gibson decided to change the design – albeit to a far more Fender-like one! We'll be looking at those later non-reverse models on the following pages, but for now here's a rundown of Gibson's original Firebird line-up…

*Guitarist* would like to thank ATB Guitars in Cheltenham and Vintage 'n' Rare Guitars in Bath

## 1 FIREBIRD I

Much like Gibson's Junior/TV, Special, Standard and Custom models represented different price points within the original Les Paul and SG solidbody lines, the Firebird range comprised four instruments at various levels of spec and ornamentation. And as per the style of Junior and TV models, the reverse Firebird I features an unbound dot inlay rosewood fingerboard and a single pickup with volume and tone controls. This particular model was also the least expensive instrument in the range with a list price of $189.50.

A Sunburst finish was standard across the board, but in order to help Gibson shake off its staid, old-fashioned image and appeal to the more forward-thinking younger generation, all Firebirds were offered in a choice of 10 custom colours for an extra $15. Along with Frost Blue, Ember Red, Cardinal Red, Kerry Green and Polaris White, these included five metallic ("Poly") shades called Golden Mist, Silver Mist, Pelham Blue, Heather and Inverness Green.

## 2 FIREBIRD III

In the same vein as the Les Paul/SG Special, the $249.50 reverse Firebird III features dual pickups with individual tone and volume controls and a single-bound rosewood fretboard with dot inlays. These models are sometimes confused with the equally twin mini-humbucker-loaded Firebird V but can be easily differentiated by their dot fretboard markers, compensated bar bridge and short flat-arm Vibrola (Firebird Vs have trapezoid inlays, a Tune-o-matic bridge and Deluxe Vibrolas as standard).

All instruments in the reverse line-up feature bespoke Firebird pickups, whereas the later non-reverse Firebird I and III models came with two and three black 'soapbar' P-90 pickups respectively. The original Firebird pickup is a unique device that evolved from the Kalamazoo-era Epiphone mini-humbucker – itself derived from the Seth Lover-designed PAF humbucker. Distinguished by its solid metal cover, it was constructed using blade magnets (as opposed to passive screws and slugs) along with inductance-enhancing ferrous reflector plates.

## 3 FIREBIRD V

In the style of Les Paul and SG Standards, the reverse Firebird V sat one step below the top of the pecking order while sporting a single-bound rosewood fretboard with trapezoid inlays and dual pickups featuring separate volume and tone controls. Although identical to the reverse Firebird III in terms of pickups and electronics, an extra $75.50 would buy you an altogether fancier guitar with a 'leaf-and-lyre'-engraved Deluxe Vibrola and a fully adjustable Tune-o-matic bridge.

In terms of body/neck construction, the reverse Firebirds utilised a unique neck-through-body design with wings glued on either side. They were, however, troublesome guitars to build and were notorious for suffering headstock fractures. An inherent weak spot behind the nut coupled with heavy banjo-style tuners (located along the treble side of the headstock) meant that breaks even occurred inside the case. Consequently, guitars with broken headstocks became so common they are often referred to as having 'Firebird disease'.

## 4 FIREBIRD VII

At the top of the line sat the $445 Firebird VII resplendent with Les Paul/SG Custom-style gold-plated hardware, three humbucking pickups and a single-bound ebony fretboard with pearl block inlays. As per the Firebird V, these flagship 'Birds boasted a 'leaf-and-lyre'-engraved Deluxe Vibrola and fully adjustable Tune-o-matic bridge. The other models in the line came with nickel-plated hardware and rosewood 'boards, but VIIs perched well above the rest with their blingier upmarket appointments and triple mini-humbucker configuration.

Famously used by Johnny Winter, Eric Clapton and Brian Jones, reverse Firebirds have a unique tone that sits somewhere between a Fender single coil and a PAF humbucker guitar. This tone is known for its midrange bite and can be up front and assertive with a good balance between thickness and sparkle. Although various reverse Firebird reissues have been released over the years, unfaithful pickup reproductions mean they don't sound quite the same as these originals.

1

2

3

4

**DAZED & CONFUSED**

# NON-REVERSE GIBSON FIREBIRDS

*Following the reverse instruments, we take a look at Gibson's second wave of Firebirds – the 'non-reverse' models…*

Gibson Firebirds first appeared in 1963 in the form of four models: the single-pickup/dot-inlay I; dual-pickup/dot-inlay III; dual-pickup/trapezoid-inlay V; and triple-pickup/block-inlay VII. With their angular geometry and custom colours, the original line-up of Explorer-like 'reverse' Firebirds was intended to tap into the zeitgeist of the forward-thinking, automobile-obsessed younger generation and compete directly with Fender in the popular solidbody market. Unfortunately, the Firebird did not rise like the proverbial phoenix as hoped. Despite its flashy looks, it failed to catch on, and shipping figures show the early reverse Firebirds had only a fraction of the SG range's success during their brief existence from '63 to '65.

To add insult to injury, the Firebird's design was hotly contested by Fender as a mirror image of its patented offset Jazzmaster and Jaguar body shapes. Furthermore, its construction made them tricky to build, transport and handle. In a recent interview, Mat Koehler, Gibson's head of product development, told us: "In '63, after the first [Firebirds] were made, [Gibson president Ted McCarty] was probably thinking, 'What did I get myself into here?!' It was a difficult build – and still is for us now."

Alas, in June 1965, a new breed of Firebirds was unveiled at the NAMM Show – the non-reverse models. Although Gibson retained the same model names, these guitars were a world apart from their reverse-style counterparts… **G**

## 1 FIREBIRD I

The reverse Firebird I features a single bespoke-designed Firebird mini-humbucker pickup adjacent to the bridge and two knobs, whereas the non-reverse Firebird I is endowed with a pair of black 'soapbar' P-90 single-coil pickups controlled by a black sliding selector switch and four knobs (volume and tone for each pickup). Unlike the reverse Firebird I, the non-reverse model came with a Gibson Vibrola tailpiece as standard. Priced at $189.50, upon its release it was the least expensive instrument in the line-up.

As per the reverse Firebird range, Sunburst was the standard finish across all non-reverse models. In addition, Gibson continued to provide customers and dealers with a range of 10 Fender-style custom colour options. These included Frost Blue, Ember Red, Cardinal Red, Kerry Green and Polaris White, as well as metallic ('Poly') shades called Golden Mist, Silver Mist, Pelham Blue, Heather and Inverness Green.

## 2 FIREBIRD III

Aside from body shape, the non-reverse Firebird III can be distinguished from its dual mini-humbucker reverse-style predecessor by its configuration of three single-coil pickups. Like the non-reverse Firebird I, this version of the Firebird III came with a Gibson Vibrola as standard. $239.50 upon release, the Firebird III offered "all the range and versatility you could ask for, plus sharpness in the treble range and depth in the bass", thanks to its ES-5/Switchmaster-style triple P-90 configuration.

The reverse 'Birds had a neck-through-body construction that was difficult and expensive for Gibson to make, and their heavy banjo tuners exacerbated the issue of headstock fractures. In the wake of Fender's CBS takeover in '65, Gibson made its move and unveiled these more Jazzmaster/Jaguar-like non-reverse designs. With a flat body, unbevelled headstock with regular bass-side right-angled tuners and a glued-in neck they were less costly to produce and, therefore, ultimately cheaper to buy.

## 3 FIREBIRD V

While the reverse Firebird V features a single-bound rosewood fretboard with trapezoid inlays, the non-reverse version was scaled back with an unbound rosewood 'board and dot inlays (as featured on all non-reverse Firebirds) and its price was reduced in '65 from $360 to $289.50. It did, however, retain its 'leaf-and-lyre'-engraved Deluxe Vibrola tailpiece, Tune-o-matic bridge and dual mini-humbuckers.

The Firebird mini-humbuckers feature a solid metal cover. As opposed to other PAF-derived Epiphone/Gibson mini humbuckers with a single Alnico bar magnet below passive slugs and adjustable pole pieces/screws, the Firebird pickup's design has a pair of blade magnet coils and inductance-enhancing ferrous reflector plates above and below both coils. With a narrower coil aperture and fewer coil windings, the midrange-focused tone is often described as somewhere between a Fender single coil and regular Gibson humbucker.

## 4 FIREBIRD VII

With its gold-plated hardware – including a 'leaf-and-lyre'-engraved Deluxe Vibrola, Tune-o-matic bridge, tuners and pickup covers – and triple mini-humbucker configuration, the Firebird VII remained at the top of the tree priced at $379.50 (a reduction in price from the $500 '65 reverse Firebird VII with its bound ebony fretboard and large block inlays).

"Here is the ultimate in a solidbody guitar," reads the Gibson catalogue. "A completely new and exciting instrument that offers all the sound, response, fast action and wide range that could be desired." Unfortunately, the guitar-buying public did not wholeheartedly agree. After Firebird sales reached their peak in '66 with around 2,500 guitars shipped (not including around 250 V-12 electric 12-string Firebirds) sales plummeted to around 750 in '67, and again to only around 275 in '68. By 1970, the range was discontinued with less than 100 Firebirds shipped in '69.

1  2

3  4

FEATURE | Epiphone

QUALITY MUSICAL INSTRUMENTS
★ *Original* ★
# HISTORIC HARDWARE
100% GUARANTEED
★★★

# EPIPHONE EPIPHANY

Gibson pumped new life into Epiphone while rescuing the brand from sinking in the late 50s. Head of product development, Mat Koehler, recounts the tale as Gibson continues to return to its source of inspiration with Epiphone

**Words** Rod Brakes  **Photography** Olly Curtis

During rock 'n' roll's fledgling years of the 1950s, Gibson was riding the wave of the electric guitar boom while Epiphone's once-feted archtops became dead in the water. Whereas Gibson flourished in the post-war years following its acquisition by Chicago Musical Instruments (CMI) in 1944 and the subsequent appointment of Ted McCarty as CEO in 1948, Epiphone embarked on a long, slow decline following the death of its visionary founder, Epi Stathopoulo, in 1943. Along with infighting, unionisation problems and a partial relocation to Philadelphia in 1953, the House of Stathopoulo (as it was previously known) stood divided. The once-proud brand, Epiphone Inc. of New York – Gibson's fiercest competitor in the revolutionary pre-war archtop era – was now a spent force. Save for one thing: it still built some of the best upright basses in the industry.

Despite its troubles, Epiphone managed to sustain an enviable reputation as a quality builder of upright basses, or 'bass viols' as they were often called – an avenue Gibson wished to further explore in the 50s while competing against Fender's game-changing Precision Bass. Ted McCarty was so impressed with the instruments that he suggested to Epiphone's president, Orphie Stathopoulo, that if ever he decided to sell the bass business, he should give Ted a call. The seed was planted in Orphie's mind, and in the spring of 1957, he did just that.

After years of struggling to stay afloat and with morale at an all-time low, he eventually keeled over and reached out to Ted for a lifeline. With more than 80 years in the American instrument-building business, the Stathopoulo family were finally bowing out.

*"Ted McCarty sent his right-hand man on a reconnaissance mission to Epiphone"*

"Looking through our archives, my favourite topic of all is Epiphone," begins Gibson's head of product development, Mat Kochler. "When I see this stuff, I realise what a creative boom it was at the time, and we're witnessing a renaissance of Epiphone right now. The Epiphone stuff really gets me going. We have memos from April 1957, when Ted McCarty sent his right-hand man, John Huis, and Ward Arbanas on a reconnaissance mission to Epiphone. Ward would soon head up the project and become the [production manager] of Epiphone, Kalamazoo. The mission wasn't necessarily to snoop on Epiphone – it was about gauging the opportunity to purchase its upright bass business. John and Ward reported back that [Epiphone] was very well equipped to be making upright basses. Ted then contacted Orphie Stathopoulo with an offer of $20,000, which he accepted right away."

While the Gibson team was busy organising transportation of the basses along with associated parts and machinery from Epiphone's New York and Philadelphia sites to its Kalamazoo factory,

74 | LEGENDARY GUITARS

Assembled in Kalamazoo, this 1959 Epiphone Coronet features an early-style slab body, 'bikini' headstock logo plate, octagonal knobs, and 'New Yorker' pickup

FEATURE | **Epiphone**

**1.** Dated 29 March 1957, this letter from Epiphone president Orphie Stathopoulo is addressed directly to Gibson president Ted McCarty and chronicles a turning point in guitar history

**2.** The slab bodies of Epiphone's seminal Coronet, Wilshire and Crestwood electrics soon gave way to a thinner design with rounded edges, as seen here on this 1961 Epiphone Wilshire

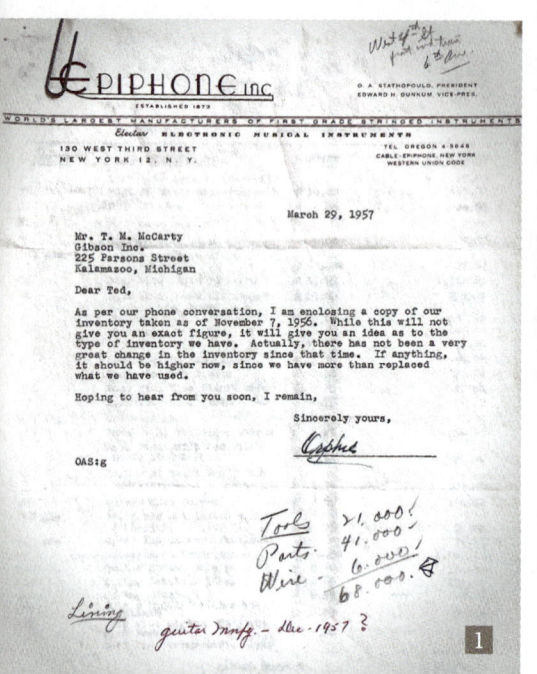

John Huis suddenly realised Epiphone wasn't just packing up the bass business.

"They were gathering up everything: basses, guitar bodies, necks, pickups – they were clearing out," continues Mat. "[Gibson] quickly became concerned about Orphie realising they may not have intended to buy everything for $20,000. John sent a hurried telegram to Ted saying, 'They think we're buying everything: guitars, amplifiers, you name it – they've pulled everything out for us to ship to Kalamazoo,' and then Ted changed course and alerted his lawyers saying, 'We need to make this happen ASAP because this opportunity is too good to pass up.' It was all orchestrated by Ted, and once everything was on the move, CMI set up Epiphone Inc. of Kalamazoo.

"There's a letter from Orphie dated 'March 29, 1957' [pictured above] where he talks about Epiphone's inventory, which was done in the previous November. Tongue in cheek, he says, 'The inventory hasn't changed since then,' basically insinuating that sales were stagnant. Its main problem was it didn't have any product direction. Gibson also floundered a little bit before '57 and '58, but Epiphone did not have solidbody guitars. There wasn't much in the way of forward-thinking designs. You could argue the same for Gibson with respect to basses; while Fender were busy creating the industry standard in electric bass, Gibson were still thinking there was a real opportunity with upright basses. But, interestingly, that's how Gibson were able to acquire their former competitor."

Although Gibson's ambition to produce a successful line of upright basses was never fulfilled, the large influx of Epiphone guitar parts inspired a radical change of direction.

"Around early to mid-1957, it became apparent they were going to be getting everything from Epiphone and [Gibson] immediately came up with the idea to create an entire product line – but not just basses," clarifies Mat. "They had already worked out what basses they wanted right off the bat, and now they were scrambling to come up with an entire product line of guitars. They were trying to make the most of the spare parts. [Gibson's] parent company, CMI, in Chicago said, 'Send us a

*"Gibson were scrambling to come up with a product line… trying to make the most of the spare parts"*

product portfolio. What does the price list look like?' Some of the names and prices were modified, but it was approved. And they consulted with Clarence Havenga, the sales manager, who said, 'Here's your in: if you come up with a product line, we can sell them in stores where we previously denied them the Gibson line because they are too close to an existing dealer.'"

With a plan in place and CMI keen to make progress, Ted McCarty whipped his team into action ahead of the rapidly approaching July 1958 NAMM Show in Chicago where the new line of Epiphone guitars was to be unveiled.

"The guitars were concepted in the early part of 1958," Mat tells us, "and in May, Ted McCarty felt compelled to send a memo with words to the effect of, 'If anybody has a problem building a guitar with Epiphone on the headstock then see me because we need this done immediately – any delay will result in serious consequences.' There was so much going on at the time and Gibson were creating their own new models. The July 1958 NAMM Show in Chicago was epic. Epiphone had their own room – number 729 – at Palmer House. Their order book was not earth shattering right after NAMM, but in a letter Ward sent to Ted recounting the event, he made a note that Forrest White from Fender stopped by to offer his 'congratulations on the

76 | LEGENDARY GUITARS

3. Ted McCarty's ambitions for the new Kalamazoo-built Epiphone range extended to the production of flat-top acoustics such as this maple-bodied FT-110 Frontier dreadnought from 1963

4. One of the lesser-known models, the E252 Broadway is a deep-bodied electric archtop, and with its dual mini-humbuckers and Frequensator tailpiece it showcases a unique Epiphone design

nice-looking instruments'. Ward thought they did pretty good.

"My favourite Epiphone story concerns the fabled Moderne. The name Moderne probably originated from that [1957 Gibson Modernistic series] patent drawing, but by the time they were submitting their ideas for Epiphone, they felt the most viable use of that name would be for the double-cutaway [Epiphone solidbodies]. Looking at this memo in front me, it appears there are two Modernes, both with poplar bodies – which is very unusual, although that does tie in with some other Ted McCarty blueprints and drawings I've found that mention poplar. It says, 'poplar body, black finish, nickel hardware, single pickup and wrap[around] tailpiece'. Clearly, that's referring to the Coronet, but it's called the Moderne. And then they've got the Moderne Deluxe. That also specifies a poplar body but with 'dual pickups, gold hardware, Sunburst finish and wrap[around] tailpiece', and that's what becomes the Crestwood. To me, the slab-bodied Coronet is one of the coolest models of all time. It hasn't yet got its due."

As the new Epiphone guitars began to catch on, sales steadily crept up in the early 60s (comprising around 10 per cent of Kalamazoo's output of instruments by 1961) and the team continued to refine the brand's identity, notably with the

FEATURE | Epiphone

**5.** In this letter from the Gibson company archives dated 2 May 1957, Ted McCarty thanks Orphie Stathopoulo for "the opportunity to work with you in liquidating the Epiphone operation"

**6.** The EB-232 Rivoli semi-hollowbody electric bass is highly regarded for its full, deep tone – courtesy of its neck-positioned humbucker – and is the Epiphone equivalent of the Gibson EB-2

---

introduction of the mini-humbucker – a dual-coil pickup derived from Seth Lover's original humbucker design.

"The reasons for the mini-humbucker are twofold," highlights Mat. "One, they were looking at what they would use on Epiphone guitars when they ran out of the old stock of 'New York' pickups; and two, they were already developing pickups for Silvertone, specifically the Chris Isaak 1446L model. We've found Seth Lover's unit cover blueprints – one for Silvertone and one for Epiphone – and they are both dated within the same time frame [spring 1961]. This blueprint was just for the unit covers, so they had probably developed the whole strategy by then. Functionally, they are the same, but the design differs slightly. They knew they wanted something unique for Epiphone, plus it was more or less the same form factor as the New Yorker pickup.

"I'd say Epiphone was a more focused product line than Gibson because they had the opportunity to start afresh. And it was apparent that they had a better strategy: Coronet, Wilshire, Crestwood; Casino, Riviera, Sheraton; Texan, Frontier, Excellente. It was really important to the guys that worked on these concepts – particularly Ward Arbanas, [demonstrator] Andy Nelson and [chief engineer] Larry Allers – that the price differences were justified visually. The Epiphone guitars sometimes looked a little bit fancier then the Gibson high-end models. The Epiphone Riviera was actually more expensive than its Gibson equivalent, the ES-335. I've heard old-timers say that Epiphone was almost considered like a custom shop – an elite team of skilled workers and designers with top sales feedback. They knew what they wanted, and they did their best to execute it."

While looking to improve its products, feedback from the sales department was considered crucial; those suggestions and requests from customers and dealers directly influenced the evolution of Epiphone guitars.

"Andy Nelson was the main consultant for Epiphone out in the field," says Mat. "He was the guy in the stores giving the clinics because he was a world-class guitarist. He would hear from dealers

•

*"We're sitting on a cache of blueprints and design files for items that were never even created"*

•

and players that would say things like, 'I could really do with a skinnier neck with a narrower nut width.' That's the kind of feedback that instigated a lot of the changes in the product line. Epiphone did those changes at least a year ahead of Gibson. Epiphone were moving to the narrower nut width and slimmer necks as early as 1963.

"Epiphone's order book was strong in the mid-60s. Kalamazoo's best year ever preceded Ted McCarty's exit [in 1966], which has always been a mystery to me. Did he see the writing on the wall? He clearly wanted out in 1965, but at the same time they were the most successful they had ever been. The Kalamazoo factory was producing more than 100,000 instruments [of which Epiphone made up around 20 per cent]. At that time, Epiphone's order book was very healthy, but, as I learned from Andy Nelson's nephew, Andy felt that the workers were deliberately not converting the order book to meet the demand.

"That was one of the things that doomed Epiphone; even though they were wildly popular, and The Beatles were playing Casinos, they just couldn't meet the demand. And I've heard that from a few other sources – there was competition between Gibson and Epiphone because Epiphone was treated differently.

LEGENDARY GUITARS

7. The E360TD Riviera semi-hollowbody electric was Epiphone's answer to the Gibson ES-335TD and was priced at $325 upon its release in 1962 (at which time the ES-335TD was listed at $300)

8. This '64 Casino belongs to Johnny Marr and was bought during a shopping trip to Denmark Street shortly after he moved to Earls Court in the 80s. The guitar was used to record the main guitar parts for The Smiths' hit *How Soon Is Now?*

[The instruments] went through the factory side by side but they were managed separately, and that kind of created a rift."

With production at a fraction of its peak by the end of the 60s, Epiphone guitar manufacturing was shipped overseas in an effort to beat the more affordable import brands at their own game, and the last of the remaining instruments trickled out from Kalamazoo during 1970.

"The reason the market peaked in the mid-60s in Kalamazoo is because immediately after that Japan started catching up and building really great lower-cost instruments," reasons Mat. "There's more demand than ever now and people are looking at more budget-friendly instruments. I'm so in love with Epiphone because of the amount of thought and energy that went into the brand in such a short amount of time. They produced some really cool ideas back in the day – many of which we haven't released yet. We're sitting on a cache of blueprints and design files for items that were never even created. We've revamped some of the old designs and they're killer. In my opinion, these new Epiphones are truly the best value electric guitars." **G**

*Guitarist* **would like to thank both Vintage 'n' Rare Guitars in Bath and ATB Guitars in Cheltenham**

*Electric*Evolution

# Epiphone Casino E230TD

Emerging alongside a Gibson rival, this humble guitar's appeal endures…

When Gibson's owners, CMI (Chicago Musical Instrument Co) acquired Epiphone in 1957, they were mainly interested in the firm's impressive range of upright basses, such as the B-4 and B-5 Artists Model. Originally based in New York, Epiphone eventually moved to Philadelphia in 1953, before the brand relocated production to Gibson's Kalamazoo premises following the acquisition. Kalamazoo-manufactured Epiphones (still noted for their desirability among players and collectors) were first showcased at a trade show in 1958, with shipping beginning the following year.

Aside from increasing CMI's export business, especially to the UK, Epiphone-branded instruments also expanded the company's domestic foothold by

> The Casino achieved greater publicity than its 'upmarket' Gibson cousin, the ES-330TD

establishing new stockists within localities with existing Gibson dealerships. Avoiding direct competition between local retailers, Epiphone dealerships were generally offered to competing music stores within the same area, with instrument prices challenging their Gibson counterparts.

However, many of these instruments often bore little difference in terms of general design to their Gibson equivalents. They were manufactured on the same production line, using the same materials by the same craftsman, and the overall difference in terms of quality, for the player, appeared relatively minor, hence their continued desirability. Epiphone's 'golden era' at Kalamazoo, however, lasted roughly a decade, as in 1969, CMI was taken over by the ECL company – soon to be renamed Norlin – and future production was subsequently relocated to Japan, marking the end of an era for this historic brand.

Conceived in the wake of Kalamazoo's Gibson ES-330TD released in 1959, the Epiphone Casino E230TD, made its debut in 1961. The comparisons between both guitars are apparent: laminated, fully hollow thinline electric archtops, sporting a single bound top and back, resplendent with f-holes on both the treble and bass sides, with double rounded cutaways and double P-90 pickups.

Controls for both guitars are virtually identical, with independent volume and tone knobs for each pickup, along with a three-way pickup selector switch. Both the Casino and the ES-330TD were originally released with dot inlays along their single-bound rosewood fingerboards, although in 1962 both received a slight alteration with the Casino changing to larger single-parallelogram inlays – the ES-330TD changed to block inlays at this point.

The Casino was originally released in a choice of either Sunburst or Royal Tan, although as the 60s progressed and custom colours gained appeal, Kalamazoo further experimented with finishes and more options became available.

Somewhat perversely, the Epiphone Casino has achieved far greater publicity by way of endorsement than its 'upmarket' cousin, and this was almost exclusively thanks to all three guitar-toting members of The Beatles.

Other notable Casino slingers include Thom Yorke, Keith Richards, Noel Gallagher, Johnny Marr and Paul Weller. **G**

## The Evolution of the Casino E230TD

**1961**
Optional vibrato; dot inlays; black pickup covers; metal badge logo; tortoiseshell pickguard

**1962**
Single-parallelogram inlays appear; pearloid inlaid script logo standard

**1963**
Nickel-plated pickup covers appear; white pickguard

**1964**
Elongated headstocks appear

**1965**
Chrome-plated hardware becomes standard

**1966**
Sparkling Burgundy finish appears (often fades with UV exposure to greenish tint)

**1967**
Cherry finish available

**1968**
Black, opaque 'witch hat' knobs become standard

**1969**
Last Casino shipped from Kalamazoo

**1970**
Epiphone Casino E230TD production officially discontinued in USA

*The Casino wound up stealing the ES-330's thunder*

*The Epiphone's long headstock is a hallmark feature*

## 1966 Epiphone Casino E230TD in Pelham Blue

**1. SERIAL NUMBER**
Six digits ink-stamped onto back of headstock; no 'Made In USA' stamp

**2. HEADSTOCK**
Elongated headstock; pearloid inlaid script Epiphone logo

**3. PLASTICS**
White pickguard; four clear bonnet knobs with metal tone and volume caps; white plastic tipped three-way pickup selector switch; nylon bridge saddles; 'slashed-C' Epiphone logo on black truss rod cover

**4. HARDWARE**
Chrome-plated, raised diamond trapeze tailpiece; chrome-plated adjustable tune-o-matic bridge set into top; three-a-side tuners with metal buttons

**5. PICKUPS**
Chrome-plated pickup covers; two single-coil P-90 pickups with adjustable polepieces; three-way pickup selector switch; four pots (two independent volume and tone controls)

**6. BODY**
16-inch wide, fully hollow double cutaway thinline; laminated back and sides with pressed maple/birch arched top; single top and back binding; super-rare Pelham Blue finish

**7. NECK**
24¾-inch scale glued in one piece mahogany neck joining the body at the 16th fret; single-bound rosewood fretboard with 22 frets and single-parallelogram inlays

*Electric*Evolution

# Epiphone Riviera E360TD

Epiphone's mini-'bucker-loaded answer to Gibson's PAF-toting ES-335

Epiphone guitars have a chequered history. During the 1930s, the New York-based firm posed serious competition to Gibson in the burgeoning jazzbox market. Unfortunately, however, following the death of company founder Epaminondas 'Epi' Stathopoulo in 1943, and in the wake of World War II, Epiphone became plagued with problems. The brand's steady decline during the post-war period eventually came to an end when Gibson's owners CMI acquired it in 1957. At the same time, Gibson president Ted McCarty was leading the Kalamazoo plant into a particularly fertile period of innovation, and while some of the most groundbreaking designs in guitar building history were developed, Gibson and Epiphone thrived under the same roof.

The ES-335T (later designated as the ES-335TD) is often recognised as being the most significant new model developed during this period. Unveiled in 1958, it pioneered a unique semi-hollow double-cutaway thinline design that set a template for all that followed. Its Epiphone-branded equivalent, the Riviera E360TD, appeared later in 1962 priced at $325 – at which time the ES-335TD was listed at $300. Although 335s command a far greater price on the vintage market nowadays, this clearly demonstrates that Epiphone guitars made in Kalamazoo were not intended as inferior instruments in terms of quality.

Aside from some typical Epiphone hallmarks including mini-humbuckers, Frequensator or Tremotone tailpieces, single parallelogram fretboard inlays, and headstock profile, Rivieras share much in common with 335s. Sporting a solid maple centre block and measuring 16 inches wide by 1¾ inches deep, both instruments feature a laminated maple body construction with single top and back binding and unbound f-holes. Additionally, both instruments have a one-piece mahogany neck that joins the body at the 19th fret, a 24¾-inch scale length, and a single-bound 22-fret rosewood fretboard.

The E360TD was originally listed with a Royal Tan finish – a bright two-tone red/yellow sunburst. This remained the model's only finish option until 1965 when a darker three-tone brown/red/yellow sunburst referred to as "shaded" was offered concurrently. By 1966, Royal Tan was no longer listed, and Cherry became a second option with the model designation E360TDC – Thinline Dual (pickup) Cherry. That same year, Sparkling Burgundy metallic finishes frequently began to appear, also labelled as E360TDC models. Although there is no mention of it in Epiphone's '66

## Aside from some typical Epiphone hallmarks, Rivieras share much with 335s

catalogue or price list, this corresponds with Gibson's price list the following year, when Sparkling Burgundy appears as a regular/non custom colour option for its thinline double-cutaways.

Aside from finish, Rivieras changed relatively little from 1962 until they were discontinued in 1969. Perhaps the most obvious change occurred in '63 when headstocks began to transition from the shorter traditional 'open book' profile to an elongated design with bevelled edges (standard from 1964). Another transition began in '64 when the 1 11/16-inch nut width was decreased to 1 9/16 inches on some models, with examples of both continuing into the following year. In 1965, chrome-plated hardware began to replace the older nickel-plated type, and from '66, black 'witch hat' knobs appeared concurrently with metal cap 'reflector' knobs.

Notable Riviera players include Stevie Ray Vaughan and Carl Wilson, who played a 12-string version after it was added to the Epiphone line in 1965. In later years, Jorma Kaukonen and The Strokes' Nick Valensi boasted their own Riviera signatures. G

## The Evolution of the Epiphone Riviera

**1957**
CMI purchases Epiphone and production relocates to Gibson's Kalamazoo factory

**1958**
Gibson ES-335T introduced (same dimensions as Riviera)

**1962**
Riviera E360TD introduced; Royal Tan finish

**1963**
Transition from short 'open book' headstock to elongated type begins

**1964**
Nut width begins to transition from 1 11/16 to 1 9/16 inches

**1965**
Riviera 12-string (E360TD-12) introduced; Royal Tan or "shaded" sunburst finish

**1966**
Cherry & Sparkling Burgundy finishes (E360TDC/-12); 'reflector' & 'witch hat' knobs

**1967**
Tremotone vibrato tailpiece (E360TDV/C); peak production (over 1,400 Rivieras shipped)

**1968**
Production declines by around 77%

**1969**
Discontinued

Guitarist would like to thank ATB Guitars in Cheltenham www.atbguitars.com

## *Electric*Evolution

### 1965 Epiphone Riviera E360TD

**1. SERIAL NUMBER**
Six digits impressed into upper rear of headstock; 'Style E360TD', 'Epiphone Riviera' and corresponding serial number ink-stamped onto rectangular blue label (visible through bass f-hole)

**2. HEADSTOCK**
Elongated profile with bevelled edges; Epiphone logo and oval 'cloud' pearl inlays; black finish

**3. PLASTICS**
Two-ply (b/w) truss rod cover with white epsilon logo; three-ply (w/b/w) bevelled edge pickguard with silver epsilon logo; two black pickup surrounds; four metal cap bonnet knobs (two 'Volume' and two 'Tone'); white selector switch tip

**4. HARDWARE**
Nickel-plated hardware: Frequensator tailpiece; ABR-1 Tune-o-matic bridge with nylon saddles; individual double-line Kluson Deluxe tuners with metal buttons

**5. PICKUPS**
Two patent number (2,737,842) sticker mini-humbuckers with nickel-plated covers; independent volume and tone controls (including four 500kohms pots and two tone capacitors); three-way selector switch; front loading jack socket

**6. BODY**
16 inches wide; 1¾ inches deep; double-cutaway thinline; laminated maple construction with solid maple centre block; pressed arched top with two unbound f-holes; single-bound top and back

**7. NECK**
One-piece mahogany; 24¾-inch scale length; 1 11/16-inch nut width; 22 frets; 19th-fret body join; single-bound rosewood fretboard; single parallelogram pearloid inlays

LEGENDARY GUITARS | 83

**DAZED & CONFUSED**

# GRETSCH CHET ATKINS SIGNATURE MODELS

### Chet Atkins will always be remembered for his golden-era Gretsch signature guitars, but can you always remember which one's which?

Chet Atkins (1924-2001) is probably the most important guitarist ever to be associated with the Gretsch guitar brand. His original line of signature models, which were launched in the 1950s, were seen in the hands of some of the most influential guitarists known to rock 'n' roll.

Eddie Cochran, Duane Eddy and George Harrison were all famous exponents of Gretsch Chet Atkins signature models in the early days, and in later years these guitars continued to be the go-to instruments for countless professional players across a broad range of styles from country, blues and rockabilly right through to hard-rock and punk.

A master of the electric guitar, gifted engineer and producer, popular recording artist and radio/TV star – Chet Atkins was as important to Gretsch as Les Paul was to Gibson. It happened to be Jimmie Webster – Gretsch's innovative guitar demonstrator and promoter – who first approached Chet in 1954 about collaborating on a signature model. As a D'Angelico archtop player and compulsive tinkerer of audio electronics, Chet certainly knew his way around a good guitar and his standards were high. From the off, he had a hand in developing the instruments that bore his name, ultimately leading to some of the most timeless designs known to the guitar world. **G**

## 1 6120 CHET ATKINS HOLLOW BODY/NASHVILLE

Chet Atkins' involvement with Gretsch began in 1954 with the 6120 Hollow Body. Although he would have significant influence on the design by requesting the addition of a metal bridge, metal nut and Bigsby tailpiece, the bulk of it was already in place by the time Chet arrived, courtesy of Jimmie Webster. Derived from the Gretsch Streamliner 16-inch electric archtop, the prototype was labelled 'Streamliner Special' and featured Gretsch Round Up-style western motifs and an 'Amber Red' orange finish.

Although he was photographed with it, Chet rarely played the 6120, instead preferring his 6122 Country Gentleman – a guitar that he had significantly more involvement in the design of from the beginning. In 1964, the 6120's name changed from Hollow Body to Nashville in reference to Chet's musical legacy as manager and producer at RCA Studio B – recording home of the 'Nashville sound' and hitmakers such as Elvis Presley, The Everly Brothers and Dolly Parton.

## 2 6121 CHET ATKINS SOLID BODY

Following the release of the Gibson Les Paul Model in 1952, Gretsch entered the solidbody market in 1953 with the single-cutaway Duo Jet. The following year, the company released two similar (chambered) solidbody models: the sparkle-finish Silver Jet and western-themed orange-finish Round Up – the latter being virtually identical to the Bigsby-equipped, maple-topped 6121 Chet Atkins Solid Body. Discontinued by 1963, this guitar is the rarest of these four Chet Atkins signature models.

Despite his status as a leading country guitarist, Chet was not a fan of the western-themed motifs of the 6120 and 6121 models and these appointments were toned down within a few years of the instruments' 1955 Gretsch catalogue debut. Although both guitars retained their orange 'Amber Red' finish, the steer head peghead inlay and steers and cacti-engraved fretboard markers were changed to a horseshoe emblem and subtler block inlays during '56, while the G-branded top logo disappeared in '57.

## 3 6122 CHET ATKINS COUNTRY GENTLEMAN

Released in 1957, the 6122 Country Gentleman electric hollowbody measures 17 inches across (a full inch wider than the 6120) and at around two inches deep was Gretsch's first thinline archtop. The 6122, 6120 and 6121 all began life as single-cutaway instruments but switched to a double-cutaway design during 1961, at which time the 6120 and 6119's large open f-holes were replaced by 6122-style simulated f-holes.

Chet was dissatisfied with the sound of the DeArmond Model 2000 ('Gretsch-Dynasonic') pickups as seen on his 6120 Hollow Body and 6121 Solid Body signature models, finding the neck pickup to be too bassy and the bridge pickup overly bright. Having worked with electronics engineer Ray Butts in the development of the Filter'Tron pickup, it was soon settled the 6122 would feature the new humbucker. The results were impressive enough that Gretsch decided the 6119, 6120 and 6121 would follow suit in 1958.

## 4 6119 CHET ATKINS TENNESSEAN

Featuring a single Filter'Tron humbucking pickup adjacent to the bridge, the 16-inch wide 6119 Tennessean hollowbody archtop was launched in 1958 and was considered a less fancy alternative to the 6120. Chet Atkins was photographed with a 6119 on the cover of his 1960 album *Workshop* and was known to favour the Tennessean as a working instrument, as did George Harrison who recorded and gigged with it during 1964 and 1965.

Unlike the other three Chet Atkins signature models featured here, the Tennessean did not change to a double-cutaway design during '61, although it did receive imitation f-holes in line with the other hollowbody archtops. At the same time, its single Filter'Tron humbucker was supplanted by dual HiLo'Tron single coils. The 6119 can also be distinguished by its 'Dark Cherry Red' and/or 6122-style walnut-coloured 'mahogany grain' finish, as opposed to the bright 'Amber Red' orange of the 6120 and 6121.

LEGENDARY GUITARS

1

2

3

4

PHOTO BY NIGEL OSBOURNE/REDFERNS

*Electric*Evolution

# Gretsch 6128 Duo Jet
Taking cues from Fender and Gibson, Gretsch released its first solidbody in 1953

Back in the early 1950s, the concept of a solidbody electric guitar was beginning to catch on. Throughout the 30s and 40s, it was the finely crafted hollowbody archtops from the likes of Gibson and Epiphone that ruled the electric roost, but that began to change when Californian upstart Fender started making waves in the guitar world.

In 1950, Fender unveiled its revolutionary Esquire and Broadcaster models, attracting reactions from sceptics who criticised the now-iconic Telecaster blueprint for its utilitarian design. To some degree, there was a reluctance to accept the new kid on the block during this watershed period in guitar history. Indeed, Fred Gretsch Jr expressed surprise at his friend Ted McCarty's decision to hit back with a Gibson solidbody electric in the form of the Les Paul in 1952. Before long, however, Gretsch followed suit. The rampant success of Leo Fender's enviable Spanish electrics was just too difficult to ignore.

Gretsch launched its take on an electric solidbody with the Duo Jet in 1953. As per Gibson's Les Paul, the model featured dual single-coil pickups (hence 'Duo') and a single-cutaway mahogany body not dissimilar to its Kalamazoo cousin. But that's where the similarities end. Whereas the Gibson Goldtop was made from solid mahogany and featured a carved maple cap, it's arguable that the Duo Jet is in fact a solidbody guitar at all. Heavily routed to accommodate cables and components, its construction is more akin to a semi-hollowbody, though a glued-on arched top devoid of f-holes gives it the appearance of a solid guitar.

Sporting a black finish, the 6128 model Duo Jet was soon joined by a distinctly more vibrant-looking equivalent model, the 6129 Silver Jet. Adorned in a silver-sparkle covering inherited from Gretsch's popular drum line, the Silver Jet arrived in 1954 along with the stained-wood finish 6130 Round-Up. Featuring an abundance of Western-themed motifs, the swanky Round-Up served as the basis for the 6121 Chet Atkins Solid Body and appeared in Gretsch's 1955 colour catalogue, *Guitars For Moderns*, alongside the new Oriental Red-finish 6131 Jet Fire Bird.

## Gretsch's seminal design was seen in the hands of the world's most groundbreaking guitar players

Although Chet Atkins tended to eschew the 6121 in favour of his 6122 Country Gentlemen signature model, Gretsch's seminal solidbody design was regularly seen in the hands of some of the world's most groundbreaking guitar players. Rockabilly guitarist Cliff Gallup was an early proponent, and rock 'n' roll pioneer Bo Diddley appeared on the cover of his 1959 album, *Go Bo Diddley*, with a Jet Fire Bird. George Harrison famously used his 1957 Duo Jet to perform and record with The Beatles during the band's early days. He later appeared on the cover of his 1987 solo album, *Cloud Nine*, brandishing the same DeArmond Model 2000-equipped guitar (referred to as 'Dynasonic' pickups in Gretsch literature).

Ubiquitous across Gretsch's electric guitar line since the late 40s, these punchy high-output single coils were superseded by the company's own Filter'Tron humbuckers in 1958. Designed by Ray Butts (inventor of the EchoSonic tape echo-equipped guitar amp) in collaboration with Chet Atkins during the mid-50s, the Filter'Tron is a completely different beast and presented the greatest change to the Jets' sound to date. The most prominent design alteration came later in 1961 when the Jets transitioned to a double-cutaway body. **G**

*DeArmond Model 2000 pickups aka Gretsch Dynasonics helped define the sound of rock 'n' roll*

## The Evolution of the Gretsch 6128 Duo Jet

**1953**
Black top; single cutaway; dual DeArmond Model 2000 pickups; block markers; script logo

**1954**
T-roof logo

**1955**
6134 White Penguin (rare)

**1957**
Hump block inlays; Cadillac Green finish w/ gold hardware (rare)

**1958**
Dual Filter'Tron pickups; 2x switches; 3x G/arrow knobs; Space Control bridge; Neo-Classic inlays

**1959**
Zero fret

**1961**
Double-cutaway; Burns vibratos replace Bigsbys

**1962**
Gold-plated hardware

**Late 60s**
Super'Tron pickups; Bigsby vibratos return; single-cutaway Roc Jet (discontinued 1980)

**1970**
Discontinued

## 1955 Gretsch 6128
## Gretsch Duo Jet

**1. SERIAL NUMBER**
Five digits typically in the 12000 to 16000 range ink-stamped onto label located in control cavity

**2. HEADSTOCK**
'T-roof' Gretsch logo; single-bound

**3. PLASTICS**
Three-ply (w/b/w) pickguard; two-ply (b/w) truss-rod cover; white-plastic heel overlay

**4. HARDWARE**
Open-back tuners with metal buttons; Melita Synchro-Sonic bridge; 'G' tailpiece; four arrow knobs; three-way pickup selector switch; two thumbscrew strap buttons

**5. PICKUPS**
Two DeArmond Model 2000/Dynasonic single coils; two independent pickup volume pots; one master volume pot (cutaway bout); one master tone pot; three-way pickup selector switch; side-mounted jack

**6. BODY**
13 ¼ inches wide; two inches deep; chambered mahogany with pressed laminated-maple arched top; single cutaway; three-ply (w/b/w) top binding; black-finish top; natural-finish back/sides

**7. NECK**
Glued-in mahogany; 24.6-inch scale length; single-bound rosewood fretboard, block inlays; 22 frets

*Electric*Evolution

# Gretsch White Falcon

Gretsch spared no expense with the launch of its flagship guitar…

**M**ost guitar builders have their pièce de résistance – a flagship model that represents the pinnacle of their craftsmanship; Gibson took Lloyd Loar's ground-breaking L-5 to the ultimate level with the Super 400 (originally labelled the L-5 Super), whilst Paul Reed Smith literally made his dreams become reality with the fantastically ornate Dragon guitars.

The jewel in Gretsch's crown came in the form of a guitar called the White Falcon. Originally intended as a one-off display centrepiece for the 1954 NAMM trade show, it ended up turning so many heads that by the following year Gretsch had put it into regular production, designated as the model 6136.

## Intended as a one-off, it turned so many heads that Gretsch put it into regular production

It was appearance as much as anything that made the White Falcon stand out from the crowd. Although the Gretsch company had set up shop in Brooklyn, New York in 1883, it certainly wasn't stuck in the Victorian era and was a notably forward-thinking firm with regards to aesthetics. In a similar vein to Fender and Gibson's infatuation with the 1950s motor craze, the angular geometry of dream cars was strongly reflected in the White Falcon's design. Stairstep tuners, a V-contoured headstock and a 'G' monogram tailpiece adorned with a V-shape reminiscent of car bonnet ornaments were all set off against a custom colour-style white finish (with more than a sprinkling of gold throughout for that aureate touch of class).

With a 25½-inch (648mm) scale length, the White Falcon measures 17-inches (432mm) across and is essentially a large, fully hollow, thinline electric archtop guitar with f-holes. It features a pressed maple top, laminated maple back and sides, a glued-in maple neck and an ebony fingerboard. These comparatively harder tonewoods lend a bright acoustic resonance to the White Falcon's natural sound and when coupled with a pair of single coil, high output DeArmond DynaSonic pickups it makes for a full, clear tone that cuts through with plenty of twang.

In 1958, a pair of noise-cancelling dual-coil Filter'Tron pickups were added, providing a little more in the way of sparkle and crunch to the overall tone. In the same year, a stereo version of the White Falcon arrived with a patented system called Project–O–Sonic, designated as model number 6137. The Project-O-Sonic design was a bold leap into the new-fangled world of stereo and although stereo guitars never really caught on, it was a sure sign of Gretsch's continued ethos of progression.

By 1962 White Falcons were being shipped with a double-cutaway as standard and it wasn't until the early 70s that Gretsch began to reintroduce the original single-cutaway version as model number 7593. In 1971, the company renumbered the non-stereo/mono and stereo double-cutaway versions to 7594 and 7595 respectively, however, in 1980 both the 7593 and 7594 models were discontinued with the 7595 being available only on special order. By 1981 Gretsch had discontinued them all.

The Gretsch White Falcon has picked up its fair share of admirers over the years (albeit most from a distance!) and is famously associated with several name guitarists including Neil Young, John Frusciante, Brian Setzer and Billy Duffy.

## The Evolution of the White Falcon

### 1954
Gretsch's Jimmie Webster unveils the White Falcon at the NAMM trade show in Chicago

### 1955
Model 6136 commences production: single-cutaway, DeArmond DynaSonic pickups

### 1958
'Thumb' inlays on fretboard, dual Filter'Tron pickups. Stereo version

### 1960
Split/double bridge mute added, detachable padded back appears

### 1962
Double-cutaway body becomes standard; zero fret appears

### 1964
Oval tuners begin to replace stairstep type; Gretsch 'G-plate' vibrato appears

### 1965
Adjustable/telescopic vibrato arm introduced; dot inlays from 15th fret

### 1971
Model numbers change to 7594 (mono) and 7595 (stereo)

### Early 70s
Single-cutaway reintroduced as model number 7593

### 1981
All models discontinued

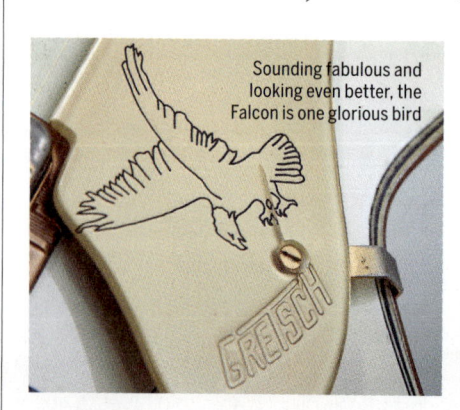

*Sounding fabulous and looking even better, the Falcon is one glorious bird*

*Stamped into nameplate on the front of headstock: "THE WHITE FALCON 36849"*

## Early 60s Gretsch White Falcon 6137

**1. SERIAL NUMBER**
Stamped into nameplate on front of headstock: "THE WHITE FALCON 36849"

**2. HEADSTOCK**
V-shaped top; horizontal Gretsch logo in gold; gold sparkle binding and V-top truss rod cover; white finish

**3. PLASTICS**
Gold pickguard with Falcon graphic and Gretsch logo; split/double foam mutes in front of bridge; white detachable back pad; white plastic rear control cavity cover; gold sparkle top and back binding; gold pickup surrounds; gold sparkle neck heel cover

**4. HARDWARE**
Gold plated stairstep tuners, Cadillac 'G' tailpiece and roller bridge; two mute knobs either side of bridge; two gold pickup volume knobs; two gold plated screw-in strap buttons

**5. PICKUPS**
Dual patent number Filter'Tron double coil pickups stamped "U.S. PAT. 2892371" with split stereo signal; four three-way tone switches on upper bass bout; three-way pickup selector switch on upper treble bout; independent pickup volume pots on lower treble bout

**6. BODY**
Fully hollow double-cutaway thinline with double bound f-holes; pressed arched maple top; laminated maple back and sides; white finish

**7. NECK**
Glued in maple neck with white finish; ebony fingerboard with 22 frets (including zero); 'thumb' inlays up to 17th fret

MARSHALL
MK II
OFF
ON
STANDBY
ON
INDICATOR
PRESENCE
BASS
MIDDLE
TREBLE
HIGH TREBLE
LOUDNESS 1
NORMAL
LOUDNESS 2
INPUTS
Marshall

# AMPLIFIERS

## DAZED & CONFUSED

# FENDER TWEED AMPS

Terry Foster, co-author of *Fender: The Golden Age 1946-1970*, imparts his expert knowledge on Fender's earliest amps

"Fender amps are rooted in Leo Fender's radio repair shop," says Terry. "By 1940, he had a full-time business with several employees in Fullerton under the Fender name. It was very successful in the local area, and, according to Leo, they did over 10,000 repair jobs in 1943 alone. Around that time, Doc Kauffman – a local professional musician and inventor – would often go into Leo's shop, which also sold records and sheet music, and they struck up a friendship. Doc came onboard full-time in 1942 and they ended up patenting a pickup [called the Direct String Pickup], so Leo used his existing knowledge of radio to adapt an amp for it. That's when Doc starts making lap steels and Leo starts making custom amplifiers.

"They also invented an automatic record changer and could have made millions, but they sold the rights and used the money to start up K&F [Kauffman & Fender], building lap steel sets with amplifiers designed by Leo and his employee Ray Massie. However, because of the war effort, it didn't really get going until November 1945. They had distribution deals and it was a relatively successful start-up, but K&F didn't last long; Doc was more risk-averse than Leo and they amicably parted ways in February 1946. Manufacturing then continued under the Fender brand."

*Vintage-guitar enthusiast and author Terry Foster is an authority on Fender through the ages*

PHOTO BY JOHN PEDEN

---

### 1 WOODIES (1946-1948)

"These are the earliest Fender-branded amps and although they existed prior to Doc and Leo splitting, Leo did advance the designs somewhat. By this stage, Leo had a line of amplifiers. There was the [4.5-watt] Princeton, which was a tiny student model with an eight-inch speaker. Then there was the single 10-inch [10-watt] Deluxe/Model 26 – it has often been said the '26' is a reference to February '46. And there was the [18-watt] Professional, which has a 15-inch speaker.

"In terms of rarity, I've only seen a handful of Princetons and a handful of Professionals. Most of the woodies you see are the mid-line Deluxe/Model 26, so that was probably their bestseller. In early '48, Leo introduced the [16-watt] Dual Professional, which is the very first Fender tweed amp. It's got two 10-inch speakers and has an angled front with a vertical metal strip. Leo was constantly moving forward trying to improve his designs."

### 2 TV-FRONTS (1948-1953)

"This first full tweed line was easier to manufacture than the woodies. It meant they could use less expensive pine – rather than hardwoods such as maple and walnut – and the wood didn't need to be finished. It was all about simple, elegant designs that were easy to service and replicate at scale. At this point in time, Leo's radio shop was selling TVs, which was the next big thing, so Leo likely took inspiration from there.

"The first TV-front samples went out in May '48. In the TV-front line, there was still a Princeton and a [1x12] Deluxe, but the Professional became the Pro-Amp, and the Dual Professional was renamed the Super. That year, the line was expanded to include the [4-watt/1x8] Champion 800 student amp [superseded by the 3-watt/1x6] Champion 600 in '49], and in '52, the [26-watt/1x15] Bassman was released to accompany the Precision Bass."

### 3 WIDE PANELS (1952-1955)

"Leo was always tweaking his designs and moving forward. The look of the amps changed for the same reason things change now: how do you promote the new stuff? It's got to look different from the old stuff. Fender were selling more amplifiers than electric Spanish guitars during this period. There are some great photos online of BB King playing Gibson guitars, but he's using TV-front and wide panel Fender amps.

"The new [15-watt/1x15] Bandmaster and [25-watt/2x12] Twin amps that were added to the line were directed at the professional musician. Audiences were getting bigger; the Western swing bands of the early 50s were playing dance halls packed with 5,000 people every night. It was big business in the South West and California. This new technology meant they could project the sound and make the same music with less people on stage, which made their business more profitable."

### 4 NARROW PANELS (1955-1964)

"The narrow panel line used less wood, but it was also another way of refreshing the look. The block logo, which appeared in 1946, is replaced by a Fender script logo in 1955, and the cloth grille is supplanted by a more robust plastic material. The narrow panels consisted of 11 amplifiers with the addition of the [10-watt/1x8 and 1x10] Harvard, [10-watt/1x10] Vibrolux, and [15-watt/1x12] Tremolux. The Tremolux came out in mid-1955 and was the first Fender amp with tremolo.

"The top-of-the-line Twin changed as music changed, meaning it got louder, going from 25 to 50 watts, then 85 watts in '58. This period from '55 onwards is the rock 'n' roll explosion. Smaller bands needed to be louder. Also, the Bassman went from 26 to 50 watts and the [5F6A] circuit became the basis for the first Marshall amp. The first [brown] Tolex amps appeared in '59, but the Champ remained in tweed up to '64."

1

2

3

4

*Amp*Evolution

# Fender 'Tweed' Bassman

The 1950s Bassman combo designs laid the groundwork for countless guitar amps

As its name implies, Fender's Bassman was designed with the electric bass in mind – specifically, the Precision Bass – though it has been wholeheartedly adopted by guitarists. Indeed, Fender's current '59 Bassman LTD amp is aimed at the six-string market, featuring in the 'Guitar Amplifiers' section of its website.

This 45-watt reissue-style amp harks back to the game-changing 5F6-A circuit (one of many versions the Bassman has appeared in since its 1952 introduction), which was the basis of Marshall's 1962 debut JTM45 amps. Although these designs are extremely similar in terms of electronics, Marshall's 12-inch Celestion-loaded, closed-back speaker cabinets create a markedly different sound to the quad of 10-inch Jensens found in 50s open-back Bassman combos. But

> Soon after the ground-breaking Precision Bass appeared in 1951, Fender developed its partner amplifier

the Bassman's set of Jensen P10R speakers (replaced by the P10Q in 1959) is a far cry from its original single 15-inch Jensen format.

Soon after the groundbreaking Precision Bass appeared in 1951, Fender developed its partner amplifier. Initially, the 18-watt 1x15 Pro-Amp was the most powerful amp in the line able to be called upon for bass duties, but the Bassman appeared the following year with an original design that included a bass-friendly ported back panel and 26 watts of power. Sporting a single channel with two inputs along with volume and tone controls, this 5B6 circuit Bassman was originally decked out in the 'TV front' style of tweed amps and changed to the 'wide panel' style in '53. In both instances, the chassis was mounted to the bottom of the cabinet, attached to the top-mounted control panel by an 'umbilical cord' of wire.

In late 1954, Fender redesigned the Bassman, introducing some major improvements with the 'narrow panel' 5D6 version. This ushered in not only the 4x10 layout but also a fixed bias output stage – meaning greater headroom and a clearer-sounding bottom-end – and dual rectification, courtesy of a pair of 5Y3GT rectifier valves. Early the following year, the 5E6 version appeared sporting dual 5U4GA rectifier valves. These twin-channel (Normal and Bright) amps feature an extended control array comprising knobs labelled 'Presence', 'Bass', 'Treble', 'Volume-1' and 'Volume-2'. By this stage, Fender openly recognised the Bassman's appeal to guitar players, as the 1955 catalogue attests: "Provides true bass amplification or may also be used for other instruments due to its widely varying tonal character." (Note: the same catalogue entry advertises the Bassman as having "50 watts" of power, but various sources, including Fender, quote the power rating as 40 and 45 watts).

In 1957, the 5F6 Bassman version heralded the arrival of yet another significant development in amplifier design with the long-tailed-pair phase inverter, further enhancing the amp's power, depth and clarity. At the same time, a Middle tone knob was added to the control panel along with two inputs per channel. Meanwhile, a single 83 rectifier valve was installed, and the long-standing 6L6 power valves were superseded by dual 5881s. Featuring a GZ34 rectifier valve, the highly influential 5F6-A circuit appeared in 1958, representing what many people consider to be the zenith of the tweed-era Fender Bassman. **G**

## The Evolution of the Fender 'Tweed' Bassman

**1952**
Fender Bassman released; 5B6 version; tweed covering; 'TV front'; 26 watts; 1x15; single channel

**1953**
'Wide panel' cabinet

**1954**
5D6 version; 'narrow panel' cabinet; "50 watts" (advertised); 4x10; dual channel (Normal and Bright)

**1955**
5E6 version; 5U4GA rectifier valves

**1957**
5F6 version; 4x inputs (2 per channel); Middle added to Treble and Bass controls; 83 rectifier valve

**1958**
5F6-A version; GZ34 rectifier valve

**1959**
Rubber 'dog bone' handle replaces leather type

**1960**
Discontinued

**1990**
Reissue Series '59 Bassman

**Current**
'59 Bassman LTD

*The original Fender script logo nameplate on Rory's 'narrow panel' Bassman was replaced by a block logo one as featured on the earlier 'TV front' and 'wide panel' amps*

*Amp*Evolution

## Rory Gallagher's 1955 Fender Bassman

**CIRCUIT**
5E6 version; 4x10 speaker configuration (two Jensen P10R/two replacements); "50 watts" (advertised); valves: two 5U4GA, two 6L6GB, one 12AX7 and two 12AY7; modded with mains transformer

**CONTROLS**
Five black plastic chickenhead knobs labelled 'Presence', 'Bass', 'Treble', 'Volume-1' and 'Volume-2' (left to right)

**POWER & CONNECTIONS**
Ground switch; fuse; power switch; standby switch; red pilot light jewel; two inputs labelled 'Bright' and 'Normal' (two channels)

**CABINET**
Pine; narrow panel; 23 ½ (W) by 22 5/8 (H) by 10 ½ inches (D); Baltic birch baffle board and two-piece dual-ported back (lower section missing); top/rear control panel cutout

**ORNAMENTATION**
Chrome control panel with white font; tweed cover; brown grille cloth (replacement); metal nameplate with Fender block logo (replacement)

*Amp*Evolution

# *Fender Reverb*

A spacious new sound springs to life at Fender

During the 1950s, as the electric guitar boomed in popularity and fresh musical styles emerged, engineers and musicians increasingly experimented with various technologies to find new and exciting ways of livening up the sound of the instrument. Gibson's leading guitarist, Les Paul, wowed listeners with his revolutionary tape techniques, while Gretsch man Chet Atkins was quick to jump onboard in 1954 with Ray Butt's tape-echo-equipped EchoSonic amp. Both were leading electric guitarists of their time and were influential in establishing electric guitar effects as a crucial factor in the evolution of popular music.

## Spring reverb is an effect that approximates the sound of reverberations in an acoustic space

Taking inspiration from tremolo-equipped amps such as the Multivox Premier 66 and Gibson GA-50T (released in 1947 and 1948 respectively) Fender released its first tremolo-equipped amplifier, the Tremolux, in 1955. Although this marked a new direction in the company's amp designs, it wasn't until 1963 with the arrival of the Vibroverb that the "expanded sound" of reverb first appeared in a Fender amp. Prior to this watershed design, Fender reverb came in the form of a standalone unit simply labelled the 'Reverb'.

Developed in collaboration with the 'king of surf rock', Dick Dale, and released in 1961, the Fender Reverb sported the Hammond Type IV spring reverberation unit at the heart of its design. Originally intended for a wide variety of applications including "guitar, accordion, microphone, phonograph" and "tape recorded program material" it became very popular among surf-rock guitarists in the early 60s, with its distinctive splashy character helping to define the sound of an era.

Spring reverb is an effect that approximates the sound of reverberations in an acoustic space, in order to add a greater sense of dimension and depth to the instrument signal. In essence, it is a form of delay, although rather than producing relatively long distinct repeats à la tape echo, a spacious wash of much smaller 'reflections' is gleaned from one or more springs with transducers at either end before being blended back in with the dry signal.

Whereas most amplifiers with onboard spring reverb tend to offer just one reverb level control, Fender Reverbs feature three parameter control knobs, namely Dwell, Mixer and Tone. By turning up the amount of Dwell, more signal is sent to the reverb tank/springs and a more pronounced effect is achieved, with a distinctive 'drip' sound becoming audible at higher settings. The Tone knob increasingly brightens up the affected portion of the signal (which can be very useful to help the reverb either sit back or come forward in a mix), while the Mixer knob allows control over the wet/dry balance or reverb level.

Originally released in brown Tolex with a wheat-coloured grille cloth, Fender later added other options to colour co-ordinate with their various amp designs including blonde/wheat, blonde/oxblood and black/silver. The Reverb unit (circuit/model 6G15) was available until 1966 and was superseded by the Solid State Series FR-1000 Reverb. In 1976, a silver-panelled version called the Tube Reverb briefly appeared before being discontinued in 1978. It wasn't until 1994 that Fender revisited the original Reverb design in its Reissue Series with the '63 Fender Reverb. Available in various finishes including brown/tan, black/silver, blonde/oxblood and lacquered tweed, it was renamed the '63 Fender Tube Reverb in 2008 and eventually fell out of production in 2016.

## The Evolution of the Fender Reverb

### 1961
Reverb model 6G15 released; 6K6GT, 12AT7 & 7025 valves; blonde & brown Tolex

### 1963
Black Tolex; black plastic strap replaces leather type

### 1966
Reverb model 6G15 discontinued

### 1968
Solid State Series FT-1000 Reverb unit released (discontinued in 1973)

### 1976
Silver-panel Tube Reverb unit released; 6V6GTA & 3x 7025 valves (discontinued in 1978)

### 1994
'63 Fender Reverb released; 6V6GTA, 12AT7 & 12AX7/7025 valves

### 2008
Renamed '63 Fender Tube Reverb (discontinued in 2016)

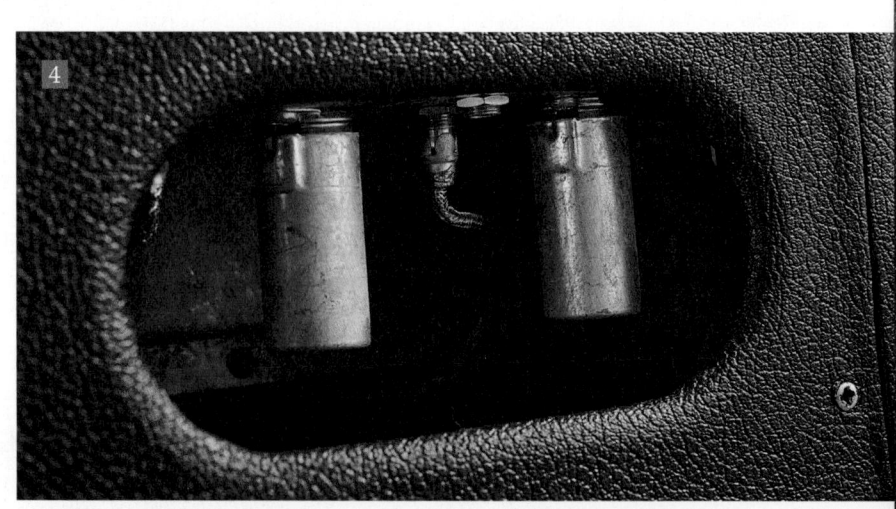

*Amp*Evolution

---

## 1966 Fender Reverb

---

### 1. CODES
Tube chart ink stamped 'PE' denoting 1966 (P) and May (E)

### 2. CABINET
19 inches wide by 10 tall by 7½ deep; vented one-piece back; control panel cutaway; four metal glide feet; one black plastic handle with two metal end caps

### 3. ORNAMENTATION
Black control panel with white font; 'Fender Reverb' script model logo; black Tolex covering; silver grille cloth; silver/black plastic Fender script motif

### 4. CIRCUIT
Model 6G15; valves: 6K6GT, 12AT7 and 7025; Hammond Type IV spring reverberation unit

### 5. POWER & CONNECTIONS
From left to right: power on/off switch labelled 'ON/OFF'; 750mA fuse labelled 'FUSE/¾ AMP'; red pilot light jewel; standard (¼-inch TS) input labelled 'INPUT'; standard (¼-inch TS) output labelled 'OUTPUT'

### 6. CONTROLS
Three white plastic barrel knobs labelled 1-10 (from left to right): 'DWELL, MIXER & TONE'; footswitch (reverb on/off)

*Guitarist* would like to thank ATB Guitars of Cheltenham

LEGENDARY GUITARS | 97

AmpEvolution

# Fender Princeton Reverb
Fender's earliest student amp graduates to pro-level status in style…

Released in 1964, the Princeton Reverb was originally brought to market as a student amp with a design largely inherited from the Princeton – Fender's first beginner amp model dating back to the brand's fledgling year of 1946. Its debut in the 1964/1965 catalogue reads: "The radically new Fender Princeton/Reverb is the result of much effort on the part of the Fender Engineers to combine in one instrument the desirable features which have been suggested by dealers, teachers and studio operators… The Princeton/Reverb with Tremolo is highly recommended for student and home use."

Although evidently aimed at students, the Princeton Reverb can be heard on countless hit records having been famously embraced by session guitarists Clarence White and Tommy Tedesco, and remains a go-to amp of many other seasoned pros including Larry

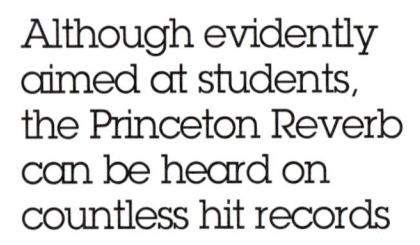

> Although evidently aimed at students, the Princeton Reverb can be heard on countless hit records

'Mr 335' Carlton and Tele aficionado Jim Campilongo. With 12 to 15 watts of power, it has long been considered one of Fender's most versatile amps whether at home or in the studio, and given the flexibility afforded by modern PA and monitoring systems, is now more popular than ever for live use, regardless of stage size.

The successful development of the Princeton Reverb didn't happen overnight; it took a long time to evolve into the giant killer combo we know today. The original Princeton, in its first incarnation as part of Fender's so-called 'Woodie' lap steel amp range, had no controls and is virtually unrecognisable from later namesake models. With a modest four-and-a-half to six watts of power and an eight-inch speaker, the early Woodie and tweed Princeton amps slowly evolved throughout the late 40s and 50s until the arrival of the "vinyl-covered" brown-panel Princeton in 1961 marked a sharp turning point in the amp's design, both in terms of appearance and spec. Rated at a considerably more powerful 12 watts and with a larger 10-inch speaker, the new Princeton boasted twin 6V6 power valves (previous versions used a single 6V6) and featured onboard tremolo, necessitating the addition of two extra knobs (speed and intensity) adjacent to the existing volume and tone controls.

In 1963, Fender introduced its iconic black-panel livery across the range, and in 1964 the Princeton's circuit was enhanced to include separate treble and bass tone controls, giving greater clarity and articulation, while increasing the number of knobs to five. The Princeton Reverb arrived that same year, featuring Fender's new onboard spring reverb for "expanded sound" alongside the Princeton's tremolo effect, requiring the further addition of a sixth knob to control reverb level. Due to an extra gain stage inherent in the reverb circuit, Princeton Reverbs appear to have less clean headroom and are known to break up more readily than Princeton amps.

In 1968, a new silver control panel was introduced and, in 1970, the rectifier valve changed from a GZ34 to a 5U4GB, resulting in less sag and compression. In 1981, the previous black-panel styling made a brief reappearance before the model was discontinued that same year.

Today, there are several vintage-style Princeton Reverb amps, inlcuding the black-panel '65 Princeton Reverb (released in 2008) and the silver-panel '68 Custom Princeton Reverb (released in 2013).

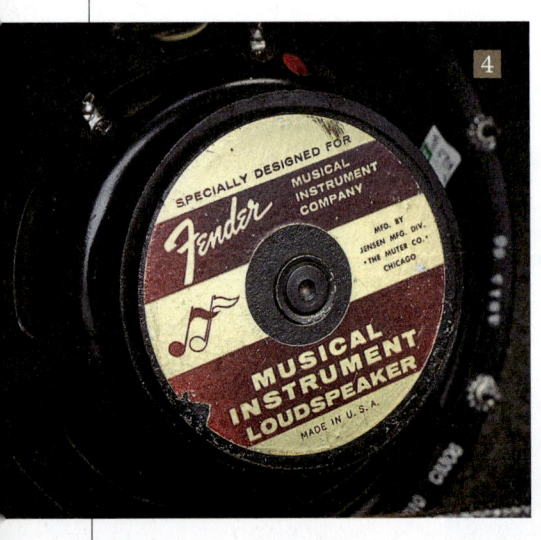

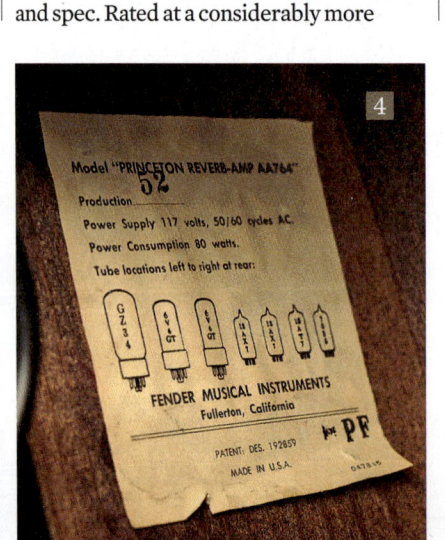

98 | LEGENDARY GUITARS

## 1966 Fender Princeton Reverb

### 1. CODES
Chassis code 'A12113' impressed into rear (normally between A05500 to A14500 during 1966); valve chart ink stamped 'PF' denoting 1966 (P) and June (F); six-digit speaker code '220617' denotes Jensen (220), 17th week (17) of 1966 (6)

### 2. CABINET
Solid pine; 19⅞ inches wide, 16 tall, 9½ deep (at base); 'vented' two-piece wooden back; angled control panel cutaway (tapering to around 7½ inches top depth); four metal base corners and glide feet; black plastic handle with two metal end caps; two metal chassis straps

### 3. ORNAMENTATION
Black control panel, white border and font; 'Princeton Reverb-Amp' script model logo; black Tolex covering; silver grille cloth; silver/black plastic Fender script motif

### 4. CIRCUIT
Valve chart reads 'Princeton Reverb-Amp AA764'; valves: GZ34, two 6V6GT, two 12AX7, 12AT7, 7025; 12 watts (minimum); one 10-inch Jensen C10N speaker

### 5. POWER & CONNECTIONS
Front: two standard (¼-inch TS) inputs labelled '1' and '2'; red pilot light jewel; rear (from left to right): ground switch, 1A 'SLO-BLO' fuse, power on/off switch, internal speaker socket, external speaker socket, vibrato switch socket, reverb switch socket, reverb output socket, reverb input socket

### 6. CONTROLS:
Six skirted metal cap black plastic knobs labelled '1' to '10' (from left to right): 'volume, treble, bass, reverb, speed, intensity'; footswitch (tremolo and reverb on/off) labelled 'Vib' and 'Rev'

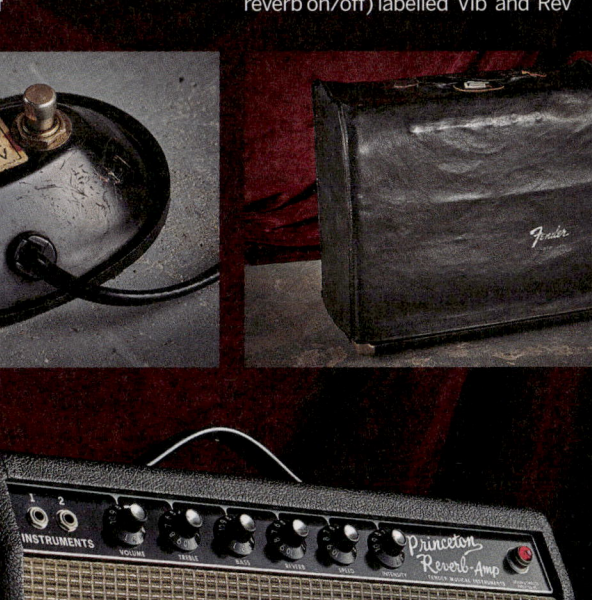

---

## *Amp* Evolution

## The Evolution of the Fender Princeton Reverb

**Mid-1946**
Princeton 'Woodie' lap steel amp released; 4 1/2 watts (min); 8" speaker; no controls

**1948**
Tweed cover; 2 knobs (volume & tone)

**1961**
Brown panel; brown Tolex cover; 12 watts (min); 10" Jensen speaker; 4 knobs; tremolo

**1963**
Black panel; black Tolex cover

**1964**
Princeton Reverb released; black panel; black Tolex cover; 6 knobs; tremolo & reverb

**1968**
Silver panel; black Tolex cover

**1970**
Rectifier valve changes from GZ34 to a 5U4GB

**1977**
'Boost' push/pull pot (volume knob)

**1981**
Black panel; black Tolex cover; Princeton Reverb discontinued

**1982-1985**
Princeton Reverb II: black panel; black Tolex cover; 20 watts (min); 12" speaker; 8 knobs

*Guitarist* would like to thank Vintage 'n' Rare Guitars (vintageandrareguitars.com)

LEGENDARY GUITARS | 99

*Amp Evolution*

# Vox AC30 Twin

Inspired by the Fender Twin, this classic British amp has a voice all its own

Tom Jennings' firm Jennings Musical Industries (JMI) had previously marketed the Univox, Vox Amplifier and 'G-Series' amplifiers before the company's first electric guitar amplifier – the AC2/30 – was developed. Appearing in late 1957, this 30-watt 1x12 combo was powered by two EL34s but never went into mass production. At the time, JMI was concentrating its efforts on the 15-watt 1x12 AC1/15 aka AC15, which was successfully released in January 1958.

In spring 1959, the 1x12 30-watt AC30 appeared. This version featured the same 1x12 speaker and square TV-front design as the AC15, but it used a pair of EL34 power valves rather than EL84s. Discontinued in 1960, it was superseded by the Fender Twin-inspired AC30 Twin model earlier that year. This advanced design utilised a quad of EL84s and was fitted with dual 12-inch speakers. Much like Fender had done years before, the AC30 Twin updated its image away from the old TV-front look in 1960, and its new split-front design established the more familiar Vox appearance that remains popular to this day.

Though the two-channel/four-input AC30/4 Twin made it to market before the three-channel/six-input AC30/6, both circuits were designed at the same time – the original schematic is dated 29 April 1960 for both. As far as the player is concerned, the most obvious difference between the two is the addition of a Brilliant channel, which, alongside the Normal and Vibrato channels, produces a brighter sound. The AC30/4 and AC30/6 were manufactured concurrently for around a year until the former was dropped from production in September 1961.

AC30 Twins were originally fitted with a pair of 12-inch Rola B024 speakers, but it soon became evident that the amp needed something a bit sturdier. Vox and Celestion eventually settled on a new design in August 1960. Known as the T.530, this now legendary bespoke speaker first appeared in a silver/pink colour referred to as "Oyster Hammer" but changed to the iconic azure "Vox blue" version within months.

In 1961, Vox developed the Top Boost tone circuit aka the "optional brilliance circuit" in an effort to reinvigorate the amp's appeal by helping it to cut through more during performances. It was originally available as an add-on 'mod', but Vox soon began fitting the Top Boost circuit at the factory. In early 1964, the AC30 Expanded Frequency

## Demand for Vox amps grew exponentially during the mid-60s with Beatlemania and the British Invasion

Fifteen/AC30X 2x15 model was released, fitted with a Top Boost as standard, while later that year two further versions of the AC30/6 were added to the catalogue, namely the Treble and Bass (the existing model was dubbed Normal). From 1961, the AC30 was also available in a head/cab format known as the AC30 Super Twin, incorporating a slant-sided design from 1964 onwards.

Demand for JMI's Vox amps was growing exponentially during the mid-60s in the midst of Beatlemania and the British Invasion. Desperate for a cash injection to help his company respond, Tom Jennings sought investment from the Royston Group. Sadly, however, after selling his controlling share, in 1967 he was ousted from the very same firm he had grown and nurtured since the early 50s. It was the end of an era.

*The plate on the rear of this 1962 Vox AC30 displays the model name, serial number and some good advice!*

## The Evolution of the Vox AC30 Twin

**Spring 1959**
AC30; square cabinet; TV-front; 1x12; 2x EL34; discontinued 1960

**Spring 1960**
AC30 Twin; 2 channels/4 inputs (AC30/4); 2x12; 4x EL84; TV-front; cream/diamond covering; brown diamond grille cloth

**Summer 1960**
Oyster Hammer Celestion T.530 speakers (previously Rola B024)

**Autumn 1960**
Also available with 3 channels/ 6 inputs (AC30/6); split-front; fawn covering

**Early 1961**
Azure blue Celestion T.530 speakers

**September 1961**
AC30/4 discontinued

**Late 1961**
Top Boost circuit available; copper panel (previously black)

**1963**
Black covering

**1964**
Grey panel; charcoal covering; black diamond grille cloth; Normal, Treble and Bass versions

**1967**
Tom Jennings leaves JMI

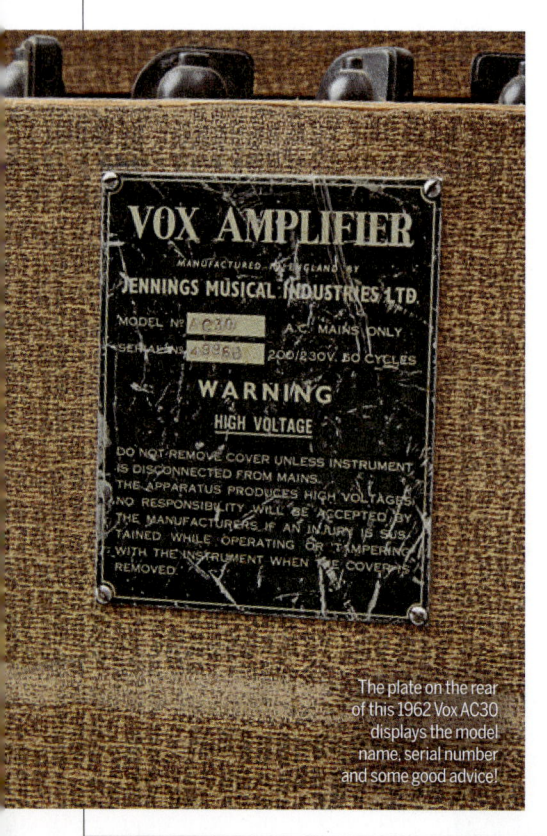

## 1962 Vox AC30 Twin

**1. SERIAL NUMBER**
Black/silver metal plate on rear stamped 'AC30' and '4996B'

**2. CABINET**
Baltic birch plywood; 27 ½ inches wide by 20 ¾ tall by 10 ¼ deep; split-front; two-piece open wooden back

**3. ORNAMENTATION**
Fawn Rexine covering; three brass vent louvres; three leather handles (originally!); white vinyl front piping; gold fascia front strip; brown diamond grille cloth; horizontal one-piece plastic Vox motif

**4. CIRCUIT**
Steel/aluminium Contempo chassis; 30 watts; dual Vox-branded 12-inch Celestion T.530 Azure blue speakers; valves: one GZ34 rectifier; one ECC82 (vibrato modulator); four ECC83 valves; four EL84s

**5. MAINS & CONNECTIONS**
Mains power switch; indicator lamp; three-amp fuse; voltage selector (115, 160, 205, 225 & 245 volts); six inputs/three channels labelled Vib-Trem, Normal & Brilliant

**6. CONTROLS**
Copper panel with six black plastic chickenhead knobs in three sections (left to right): Vib-Trem Speed and Depth; Vib-Trem, Normal and Brilliant Volumes; Tone

*Amp*Evolution

# Marshall JTM 45 MK II
How Marshall's debut amp opened a new chapter in rock 'n' roll history…

Jim Marshall's musical instrument shop in Hanwell became a hub for electric guitarists soon after opening its doors in July 1960. Responding to customer requests for a new powerful amp design and in an effort to create a more affordable homegrown alternative to expensive US imports, by September 1962, the firm had prototyped its own edgier-sounding take on Fender's 5F6-A Bassman. It featured a pair of war-surplus 5881 power valves, three ECC83 preamp valves and a GZ34 rectifier valve.

Production commenced from the end of 1962 as the team – consisting of electronics engineers Ken Bran, Dudley Craven and Ken Underwood – fulfilled a steady stream of orders for Lead, Bass and PA versions of its new amplifier, which was soon being fitted with a pair of British-made KT66 power valves. Although none of these germinal Marshalls were labelled as 'MK I', shortly after the amp's initial release, a move to wider-input jack spacing and the elimination of a Bassman-style polarity switch on its front panel (constructed of aluminium or white plastic) saw them branded 'JTM 45 MK II' in reference to Jim and his son Terry, along with the amp's ambitious 45 watts RMS power rating.

Several cosmetic permutations of the amp emerged over time, but the earliest versions can generally be distinguished by their white fabric fronts and red-on-silver capitalised Marshall-logo metal badges (known as 'coffin badges' on account of them being sourced from a funeral hardware merchant). The first few of these seminal examples feature an offset chassis and all-white front, although the amp soon adopted its more familiar symmetrical appearance with a centralised front panel and logo. For a brief period thereafter, they continued to appear with an all-white front before changing to a two-tone black-and-white design in 1963 (referred to as the 'sandwich front') and, in 1964, Jim and co finally settled upon the classic Marshall all-black livery.

With orders increasing exponentially, in June 1964, Marshall opened its first factory operation in Hayes, Middlesex – initially enabling the company to quadruple its output to around 20 units per week – and, over the following months, the JTM 45 MK II continued to evolve. Gold Plexiglas front panels appeared and the logo changed twice – first to a larger red-on-silver, then black-on-gold, Plexiglas design in block

> The earliest versions can be distinguished by their white fabric fronts and red-on-silver Marshall logo

letters. This was followed, in late 1965, by the introduction of Marshall's now iconic script logo set in white plastic (at this time embellished with either gold or silver plating). The distinctive Marshall look was now complete.

In 1965, the JTM 45 MK II received separate model number designations for each available application, including the PA (1985), Bass (1986) and Lead (1987) units, and a fourth version – the Organ amplifier (1989) – was added to the range. However, in early 1966, a new breed of 50-watt designs featuring EL34 power valves and solid-state rectification signalled the beginning of the end for Marshall's inaugural JTM 45 MK II range and it was soon phased out as the new era of hard rock began to take shape.

## 1964 Marshall JTM 45 MK II (Bass model)

### 1. CODES
'Bass' scratched into rear panel; normally 'SER' prefixed four-digit serial number (beginning with '2' in 1964) and Lead/Bass/PA designation stamped or scored on rear panel

### 2. METALWORK
Aluminium front panel with black lettering branded 'JTM 45' (on right) & MK II (on left); aluminium rear panel; 2½-inch aluminium chassis with external cabinet anchors

### 3. CIRCUIT
Perforated Tufnell circuit board; two KT66 power valves; one GZ34 rectifier valve; three ECC83 preamp valves (including one phase splitter); Radiospares RS De Luxe output transformer (30 watts maximum rated output); 45 watts RMS power rating; one 500pF Bass model voicing capacitor

### 4. ORNAMENTATION
Black Tolex cover; two-tone black-and-white 'sandwich' front; gold front strip; metal 'coffin badge' with red-on-silver capitalised Marshall logo; four original black-plastic vee knobs (two replacements); leather handle

### 5. POWER & CONNECTIONS
Front (from left to right): chrome baton power and standby switches; round amber indicator light; four instrument inputs comprising two 'High Treble' (channel 1) and two 'Normal' (channel 2) sockets. Rear: single speaker cable socket (for use with 16 ohms speaker cabinet); Bulgin power cable socket; 2A fuse

### 6. CONTROLS
Front only (from left to right): 'Presence, Bass, Middle, Treble, High Treble/Loudness 1, Normal/Loudness 2' (all labelled 0-10)

*Guitarist* would like to thank Vintage 'n' Rare Guitars (vintageandrareguitars.com)

---

## The Evolution of the Marshall JTM 45 MK II

### September 1962
Prototype developed; 2x 5881, 3x ECC83 & 1x GZ34 valves

### Late 1962
2x 5881 or KT66, 3x ECC83 & 1x GZ34 valves; all-white front; red-on-silver metal badge logo

### Early 1963
'JTM 45 MK II' branding; no polarity switch on front; wider-input jack spacing

### 1963
2-tone black/white front

### Early 1964
2x KT66 power valves standard

### Mid-1964 to mid-1965
All-black front; gold Plexiglas front panel; red-on-silver then black-on-gold Plexiglas logo

### 1965
Park 45 (rebranded Marshall JTM 45 MK II) available

### Late 1965
Plastic script Marshall logo; metal cap knobs standard

### 1966
Discontinued

### 1989
JTM 45 Lead amp reissued

## DAZED & CONFUSED

# MARSHALL AMPS

From JTMs to JMPs and JCMs, Marshall's product specialist, Steve Smith, tracks the evolution of these iconic amps

"The JMPs were born in the Plexi era – which is generally thought of as being the period from the mid-60s up until the 70s when we were using Plexiglas plastic panels," Marshall's product specialist, Steve Smith, explains. "When Marshall first began building amps in the early 60s, we had the JTM 45s. And then in the mid-60s, 50- and 100-watt amps appeared, which evolved from the JTM 45 – the model 1987 being a 50-watt amp, and the 1959 model a 100-watt amp. Both of these models were originally available right up until 1981, although there aren't many of the later ones around because people weren't asking for them by then.

"There were so many variations of amps that it can get confusing," Steve tells us. "For example, the model 1992 – as used by Lemmy – was the bass version of the 1959, but from the front it just looked like a 1959 model. So on the back it would say Super Bass, whereas the 1959 was labelled Super Lead.

"Although people tend to think of the JMP amps as models from the 1970s, the first time JMP actually appeared on an amp was a few years before in 1967. That's when you first saw JMP written on late-60s Plexis such as the 1987 and 1959. Essentially, they're the same as before, even though the name was different."

*As Marshall's product specialist and demonstrator, Steve Smith knows his JMPs from his JCMs*

### 1 JMP

"JMP stands for Jim Marshall Products – the amps that came before were labelled JTM, which stands for Jim and Terry Marshall. It was in 1975 when Marshall introduced the first 'master volume' amps. And those are often what people refer to as a JMP. Even though we had amps with JMP written on them before, it's more the 70s styling and look that people associate with the JMP name.

"When Marshall introduced the first master volume amps in '75, they used the 50-watt 1987 and 100-watt 1959 as the basis for the new 2204 and 2203 amps [respectively]. At the same time, the 1987 and the 1959 were available in the Standard series. In '76, the cosmetics changed at the request of the distributor, Rose Morris. And that's when the larger logo, white piping and illuminated rocker switches appeared. That lasted until 1981 when the JCM800 range came out."

### 2 JCM800

"By the 80s, everyone seemed to want a Marshall stack. JCM800s appeared in 1981 after Marshall's 15-year deal with Rose Morris ended, which Jim Marshall was very happy about as it meant that Marshall could distribute independently. Rose Morris had warehouses full of stock when the deal ended, so Marshall made all the JMPs obsolete by revising the look with the JCM800 line. JCM800 amp heads are recognisable by the full-width panel and cloth front, rather than the JMP-style vinyl front.

"There's not much difference between the JCM800 and JMP circuits, however. In fact, you could still get the 2204 and 2203 master volume models, and for a short while you could also get the 1987 and 1959. JCM stands for James Charles Marshall. There's no concrete answer as to where the '800' part came from, but he did have an old Jag with the license plate JCM 800."

### 3 SILVER JUBILEE

"The Silver Jubilee models came out in 1987 to commemorate 25 years of Marshall and 50 years of Jim Marshall being involved in the music industry. These anniversary amps were a limited run, but by popular demand we brought them back. They can be an acquired taste, but some well-known players use them, like John Frusciante, Joe Bonamassa and Slash. They're very comfortable amps to play, and the diode clipping means you can get saturation at a much lower volume. Rock players love them, but the clean is really nice, too. Wayne Krantz uses a Jubilee clean. Marshall clean tone is very much underrated – and it's great for pedals, too.

"This was the first time where you could attenuate the power output and there were two push-pulls on the panel: the Rhythm Clip turned the clean channel crunchy, and the other push-pull allowed you to change channel (also footswitchable)."

### 4 JCM900

"The JCM900 series evolved from the JCM800 series in 1990. Marshall realised that a lot of people were getting their amps modded as more and more came in for repair. Coming out of the late 80s it was all about more gain, and 900 series amps were popular in the grunge and indie scene. At that time, that's what people were chasing. The gain control goes to 20 on the 900s, the others go to 10.

"JCM900s don't have the same bottom-end and growl as the JCM800s and the 900s tend to sound brighter and more scooped as well. There were two main models available: the 2100 Hi Gain Master Volume MK III and the 4100 Hi Gain Dual Reverb. The 2100 is a single-channel amp with no reverb and two master volume controls. The 4100 was the more popular of the two. It has two channels – clean and overdrive – and a reverb for each."

1

2  3

4

**DAZED & CONFUSED**

# ORANGE AMPS

This British brand has spawned many a classic design
since arriving on the scene in the late 60s

The roots of British amp giant Orange can be traced back to the West End of London where, in 1968, company founder Cliff Cooper opened up a small secondhand instrument store called the Orange Shop. Having painted the shopfront a dazzling psychedelic orange colour, Cliff's new enterprise certainly caught the eye of passing guitar shoppers as they perused the wares of Soho and Tin Pan Alley.

"Guys like Marc Bolan, Gary Moore and Paul Kossoff would sit in the shop chatting and jamming all day long," Cliff told us. "It was part of the whole thing that was happening. They'd come in, take a guitar off the wall and plug in."

One such patron of the Orange Shop was a young Peter Green whose stellar guitar playing in his band Fleetwood Mac had set the London blues scene alight – and Cliff went to see them play at every opportunity. With the band on the verge of international success, Cliff offered to supply them with a full backline of Orange amps for their upcoming American tour.

"Fleetwood Mac were really the first band to use Orange equipment," said Cliff. "We were lucky. When they took our gear to America, it launched us in the States, and not too long after that, Stevie Wonder also used the equipment to record *Superstition*. That launched us all over the world."

## 1 LATE 60S

By the time Cliff had decided he wanted to build his own guitar amplifiers, he had already studied electronics at college. Working in collaboration with Mat Mathias of Radio Craft – a radio repair shop in West Yorkshire – the first Orange amps were assembled in Mat's native Huddersfield and were also branded Matamp. Meanwhile, the first Orange speaker cabinets were constructed in the basement of Cliff's shop (where, in the early days, he would often sleep!).

From November 1968, fewer than 50 100-watt OR100 Orange Matamp units were completed, making them highly sought-after collector's items. The very first amps were supplied to Peter Green's Fleetwood Mac for their US tour. The 200-watt OR200 appeared later in March 1969 and was powered by four 6550/KT88 valves (double the number onboard the original OR100). That spring, the second version of the OR100 appeared and it came fitted with four EL34s, while the new 50-watt OR50 was driven by two EL34s.

## 2 PICS ONLY

Demand for Orange amps ramped up quickly and, in early 1970, production shifted to a larger facility in the Huddersfield area with subcontractors HH Electronics and Howells Radio helping with the workload. Within a year, however, manufacturing had relocated home to the West End. And there it stayed until 1973 when Orange escalated to assembly-line production at its new factory in Bexleyheath, Kent.

Designed in 1971, the EL34-powered 'Pics Only' GRO100 and GRO50 amps were launched in 1972. Boasting crunchy overdriven tones, they were the genesis of the 'Orange sound', becoming the benchmark for all future Orange amp designs. They had a different circuit than previously and they introduced Orange's unique six-position FAC midrange tone switch. Later named the OR100, OR80 and OR120, these 'Pics Only' amps were rejigged in 1973 to include text on the control panel. The later 'Pics & Text' amps launched in 1974, comprising the classic OR120 and OR80 models.

## 3 AD SERIES

Manufacturing of the amplifiers at the Bexleyheath factory ended in 1979, though Cliff hung on throughout the next decade building and selling Orange amps – albeit in limited numbers. In 1993, the Orange brand was licensed to Gibson who opted for the new amps to be made in England by Matamp. However, these 70s reissues were not a great success (though Noel Gallagher used an Overdrive 120 model for a time), and in 1997 Cliff regained control of the brand he started back in the late 60s. It was the dawn of a new era for Orange.

Beginning with the launch of the AD30 in 1998 (an amplifier that was famously played by Jimmy Page, Adrian Utley and PJ Harvey, to name just three), Orange went from strength to strength as the AD15 picked up the Editor's Pick Award in *Guitar Player*, when it was released the following year. This new phase for the company also saw Orange reconnecting with its Fleetwood Mac heritage when the AD15 combo became guitarist Jeremy Spencer's amp of choice.

## 4 ROCKERVERB

Launched in 2003, the original Rockerverb was Orange's first high-gain amp design, making it a firm favourite in the metal world. Its versatile design also proved a winning formula for guitarists who desired an ultimately flexible amp to cover all bases. Indeed, Orange Rockerverbs are popular among sessions players for use on stage and in the studio.

After Orange began receiving requests to build an effects loop into the AD30, the company instead decided to design a new amp from the bottom up. Featuring a valve-driven effects loop (the first amp of its kind, no less), the Rockerverb 50 and 100 amps were revamped in 2010 with the launch of the MKII versions, though their much-loved Pics Only-style crunch character was retained.

The current incarnations of the Rockerverb – the MKIII amps – are available in orange and black livery and feature selectable output power options. As per the 'MKI' and MKII Rockerverbs, a combo version of the MKIII is available.

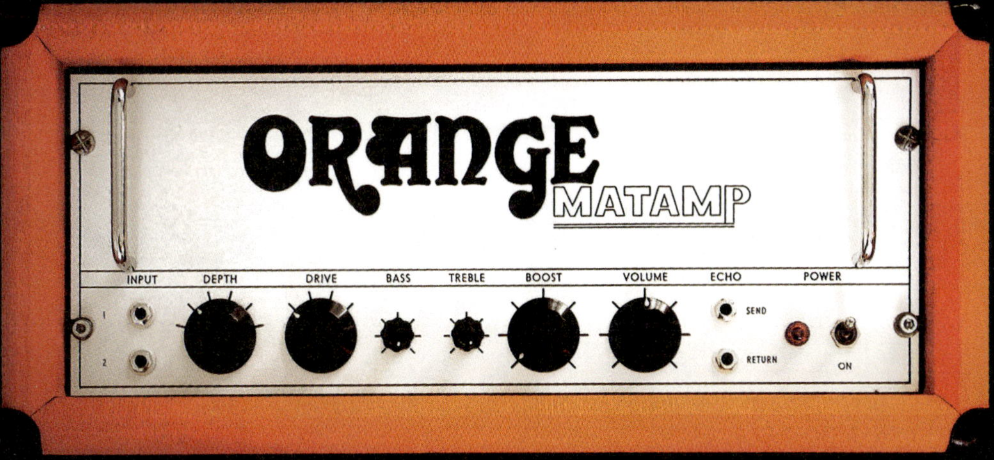
ORANGE
MATAMP
INPUT
DEPTH
DRIVE
BASS
TREBLE
BOOST
VOLUME
ECHO
POWER
1
2
SEND
RETURN
ON
1

ORANGE
2

ORANGE
AD30
Twin Channel
POWER
STANDBY
CHANNEL
MASTER
TREBLE
MIDDLE
BASS
GAIN
INPUT
TWO
ON
PLAY
ONE
3

ORANGE
ROCKERVERB 100
MKIII
FULL
STANDBY
ON
HALF
4

# ACOUSTIC GUITARS

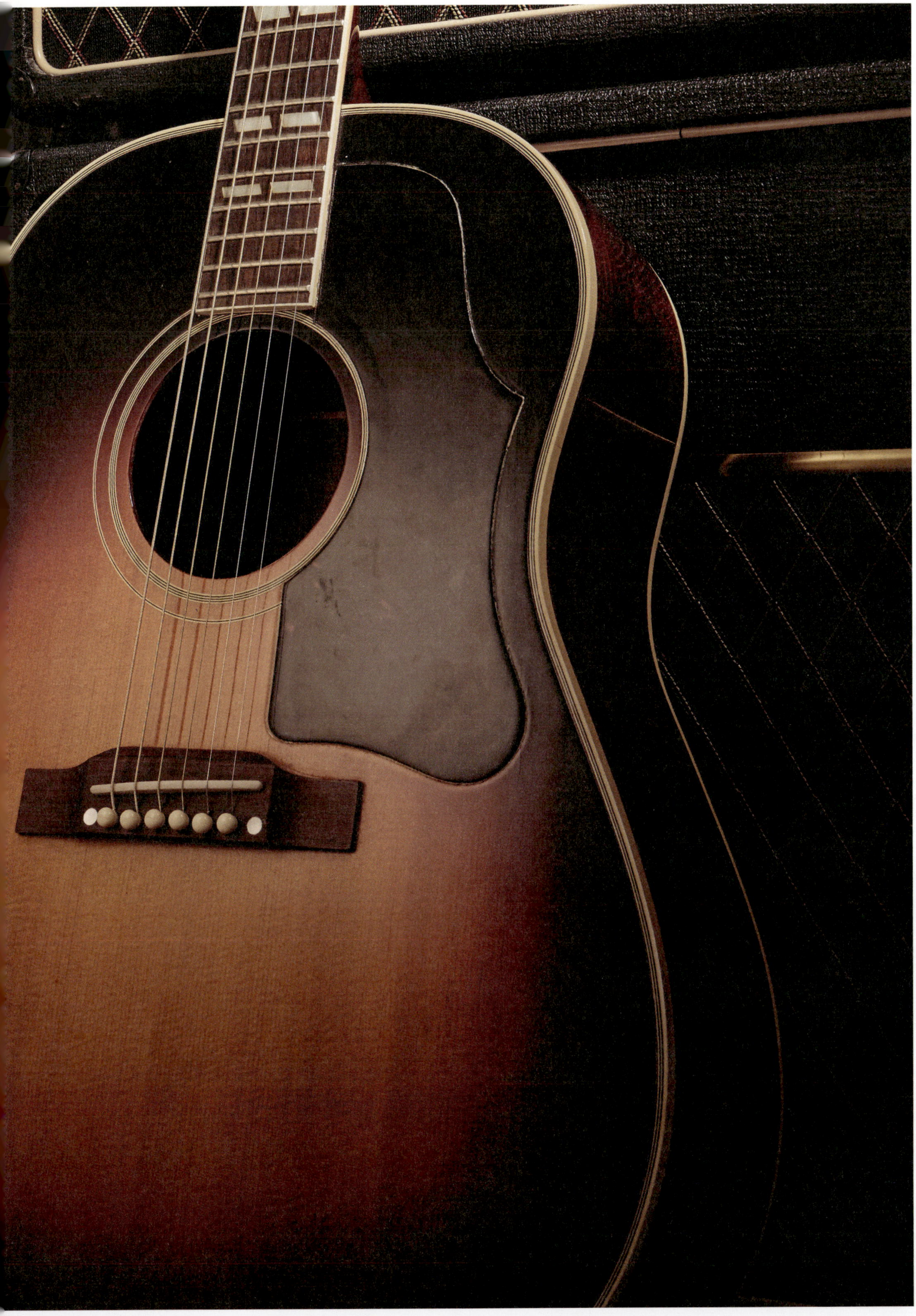

FEATURE | **19th & 20th Century Martins**

## QUALITY MUSICAL INSTRUMENTS
### *Original*
# HISTORIC HARDWARE
#### 100% GUARANTEED
★★★

# CENTURY OF PROGRESS

We take a look back at the pioneering craftsmanship of Martin's first 100 years – from the company's earliest known guitar of 1834 up to the groundbreaking arrival of the classic American 14-fret Dreadnought in 1934 – with Martin & Co's museum and archives specialist Jason Ahner

**Words** Rod Brakes  **Photography** Olly Curtis

The X-braced, steel-string, 14-fret neck, large-bodied American flat-top is an icon of modern times. It is the people's guitar – the genre-spanning voice of generations. But it took many years of experimentation and ingenuity before Martin finally evolved the instrument in the late 1920s and 30s into what many consider to be the pinnacle of acoustic guitar building. For that reason, the basic design hasn't changed much since then. Indeed, there has long been a common emphasis on looking back to the pre-war period of production as a benchmark for quality.

The story of Martin guitars begins in 1796 with the birth of company founder Christian Frederick Martin Sr in Markneukirchen, Germany. Around this time, the instrument as we know it today with six single strings was just becoming established in Europe as luthiers increasingly shifted away from building the earlier-style double course-stringed baroque guitars during the latter half of the 18th century.

"When CF Martin Sr was born, the six-string guitar was a rather new development," CF Martin & Co's museum and archives specialist, Jason Ahner, tells us. "At some point in the 1700s, they figured the guitar should have six strings and the idea eventually stuck.

"CF Sr's grandfather and great-grandfather were violin builders. We don't know why his father never got into that, but he was a cabinet maker and part of the cabinet maker's guild. He also built guitars and he saw that his son had an interest in building guitars, so he approached the violin makers to see if Christian could apprentice under them, but they declined saying they thought the guitar was a passing fad. That's when his father arranged the apprenticeship with [renowned Viennese guitar builder] Johann Stauffer. As the story goes, CF Martin Sr travelled to Vienna to get his formal apprenticeship under Stauffer when he was 15 years old. He eventually became the foreman of Stauffer's shop."

While in Vienna, CF Martin Sr married singer and harp teacher Ottilie Kuhle, and the pair relocated to Germany soon

•

*"The earliest known Martin is a shorter-scale gut-string with a sweet, mellow sound. It's still very playable 186 years later!"*

•

after their first child, Christian Frederick Martin Jr, arrived in 1825.

"He decided to move back to Germany," continues Jason. "I guess the idea was that CF Sr would set up shop building guitars there and they would live happily ever after. But there was a constant battle with the violin makers guild who claimed they had the sole right to build any stringed instrument. These battles went on for a few years and the court sided with CF Sr every time because there was no mention of the guitar in the guild articles. Plus, the guitars Christian was building were the best they'd ever seen. When his father passed away, however, he decided he'd had enough. He wanted a new opportunity."

Setting his sights on the Land of Opportunity, CF Martin Sr gathered up his young family and boarded a US-bound ship on 9 September 1833.

"They left Germany and arrived in New York City on 6 November," recounts Jason. "Imagine being in a boat on the Atlantic Ocean for two months! But right away, CF Sr went to work building guitars. For the first six years, they were in Lower Manhattan on Hudson Street. I guess the shop officially opened in May 1834. That's when you first see the label that's in this Stauffer-style guitar [pictured right]. That is the earliest known label. This is the earliest known Martin to exist. We just refer to it as 'the oldest Martin'

*110* | GUITARIST SUMMER 2020

This is the earliest known Martin guitar. Dated to May 1834, it was hand-built in New York City by company founder CF Martin Sr after he arrived from Germany in November 1833

FEATURE | **19th & 20th Century Martins**

**1.** Minimal bracing includes one brace just below and a 'popsicle' brace above the soundhole – something Martin returned to in the 1930s after steel strings became standard

**2.** Inlaid by hand by CF Martin Sr, these heart-shaped mother-of-pearl inlays and moustache bridge designs are inherited from the earlier style of 4/5 double course-string baroque guitars

or 'the Stauffer Martin', even though we have quite a few guitars with the Stauffer-style Viennese scroll headstock. It's a shorter-scale gut-string, and is very lightly built. It has a sweet, mellow sound. The great thing about this guitar is that it's still very playable. Even 186 years later! It's very similar to a Legnani model that Stauffer built. Luigi Legnani was a famous Italian guitarist and Stauffer built instruments for him. Stauffer was the one to patent that scroll-shaped headstock and the clock key adjustment in the neck. Paul Bigsby and Leo Fender later used that style of headstock on their solidbodies and a lot of people think that's where they got the idea from.

"The features on this guitar are very similar to what CF Sr would have built in Vienna. A lot of his guitars had the same type of headstock and neck construction with the clock key adjustment in the neck. It's kind of like an early truss rod; it raises or lowers the neck and adjusts the height of the strings. The moustache bridge is another Viennese build aspect. Ebony bridges – and fingerboards – were standard for Martin from the beginning. It has mother-of-pearl inlays on the edges, the little heart inlays, and just above the bridge pins. Then you have the mother-of-pearl [soundhole] rosette. There are also mother-of-pearl inlays just in front of the nut. It's an ivory nut.

"The saddle is fretwire, so it's nickel silver. That was common on a lot of early guitars. The maple neck is stained black and it has ivory strips inlaid into it, and the neck and body are bound in ivory. That wouldn't be acceptable now! And, of course, the top has the marquetry that Martin has been known for down the years. CF Sr would have done those inlays himself. It always blows me away to think he built these guitars so perfectly without any powered equipment – everything was cut and routed by hand."

As per the majority of Austrian and German guitars built during this time, the back and sides of the earliest Martin are constructed of maple in the tradition of violin makers. In New York City, however, CF Sr would soon get to grips with Spanish-style rosewood guitars as he routinely repaired cracked instruments that had fallen foul of the cold, dry north-east US winter.

"CF Sr was probably getting a lot of Cádiz guitars coming through his shop, so he could see how popular these Spanish models were," reasons Jason. "You see his designs evolve away from what he was building in Vienna and Germany to more of a Spanish-influenced guitar. Eventually he would get to know [Spanish guitarist] Madame de Goñi, but at that point it was quite a localised East Coast market.

"During this period, he was building a lot with Henry Schatz, a friend from Germany who had come over to the United States in 1832. He was the influence behind Martin moving to the Nazareth area [in Pennsylvania]. CF Sr had thought about going back to Germany, but after his wife went to visit the Schatz family just north of Nazareth, they decided to move to Cherry Hill [in Pennsylvania].

"Most of the guitars CF Sr built in New York City have the Stauffer headstock and figure-of-eight body shape, but in the late-1830s, you start to see the Spanish influence. That's when he starts building guitars with square tapered headstocks and bodies with a narrower upper bout. Eventually, he came up with the pyramid bridge and then used that almost exclusively. I think he got the basic idea from the rectangular bridges on

*"It always blows me away to think CF Sr built these guitars so perfectly without any powered equipment – everything was by hand"*

Spanish guitars, but the pyramid bridge and the later belly bridge [from 1929] are both styles that Martin came up with."

As CF Sr continued to explore the Spanish style of guitar building, he began using the typical fan bracing, although soon discovered it was incompatible with Stauffer-style pin bridges.

"Spanish guitars use a tie block bridge," Jason points out, "but CF Sr wanted to stick with pin bridges because he liked the design. The problem was he would hit the fan braces when he was drilling the pin holes, so he started trying different things. In the late 1830s and early 1840s, you see variations between fan bracing and traverse tone bars, and then a kind of X-brace system. Finally, in 1843, you get the Madame de Goñi guitar – the first X-braced Martin. It's kind of like a double 'X', which is a little different to the 'mature X-bracing' we use now. He first started using that a little later in the 1850s. Madame de Goñi was probably the most prominent guitar player in the US during that time, and her [size 1] guitar was the largest model Martin were building back then. After he built that guitar, he started building larger models like it regularly. His dealers at the time just began ordering 'the de Goñi model'. They'd say, "I want a size 1 de Goñi". In a way, Madame de Goñi was Martin's first signature artist!"

3. CF Martin Sr was an apprentice of Viennese guitar builder Johann Stauffer and these iconic Stauffer scroll headstock designs carried over to the earliest Martin guitars of the 1830s

FEATURE | **19th & 20th Century Martins**

4. Ivory pyramid bridge and mandolin-style pickguard: pickguards first appeared on special order guitars around the turn of the century but didn't become standard until the 1930s

6. 'Fern' headstock inlays featured on early style 45 models. 'Flowerpot/torch' inlays were used thereafter, until large pearl CF Martin logo inlays became standard in the 1930s

5. Most models switched to 14-fret necks during the 1930s, but 12-fret necks and slotted headstocks remained standard features on 0-42 and 00-42 guitars until their discontinuation in 1942

With greater perceived volume and low-end power, the demand for larger-bodied guitars continued.

"You see the first 0 size in the sales ledgers in 1854, followed by the first 00 size in 1858," highlights Jason. "After that, Martin didn't build anything larger until 1902 when you see the first 000 size – a 000-21. By that stage, guitar players wanted to join in with mandolin and banjo clubs, so they needed more volume and, therefore, larger instruments. Martin started building mandolins in 1895 and the intricately inlaid style of the 6 and 7 models then crossed over to guitars in the late 1890s. Before that, Martin were really conservative with their inlays. Even the style 42 – which was Martin's top-of-the-line until 1904 when the first style 45 was offered – only had position markers at the 5th, 7th and 9th frets. The guitar pictured is a late-1901 00-42S. It's a transition model between the style 42 and what would soon become the style 45. Back then, the 'S' just meant 'special'. It was kind of like their custom shop at the time.

"It has an ivory bridge, which is something you would see on styles 34 and above up until the late 1910s when Martin stopped using ivory for bridges and binding. I believe the pearl-inlaid tuning machines on this guitar are also ivory, as is the binding on the body and neck. There's some gold inlay on the headplate, but for models like this, Martin didn't do the inlay on the headplate, fingerboard or pickguard; there was a shop in New York City they would order these from. It's got an Adirondack spruce top, Brazilian rosewood back and sides, and a two-piece cedar neck. The headstock was grafted to the barrel, which is where the carved diamond volute comes from on style 28 guitars and above. This one is another gut-string model, so you're not going to get the projection you do from steel strings, but it has a really great sound."

After its first steel-string model appeared in 1902 (a special order 00-21), Martin began offering steel-string guitars in the 1910s when Hawaiian music was popular, and in 1922 the first production model to be offered with steel strings only – the 2-17 – appeared.

•

*"Hawaiian music was king in the 1920s. That's when you see steel-string guitars start to cross over to other genres of music"*

•

"Steel strings came from Hawaiian music and Hawaiian music was king in the 1920s," emphasises Jason. "That's when you see steel-string guitars start to cross over to other genres of music like early blues and country. Around 1927, Martin started offering steel strings as standard and gut strings as special order instead. Hawaiian music changed everything because they needed even more volume. That's where you see the Dreadnought eventually come in. Martin built the model for [Hawaiian musician] Mekia Kealaka'i and then they built the Dreadnought for Ditson based on that in 1916.

"But the Dreadnought really comes into its own in 1934 – that's when you see the first 14-fret neck Dreadnoughts appear. The 1929 OM-28 was the first 14-fret neck Martin guitar, and a lot of people consider that to be the first modern flat-top acoustic guitar," Jason tells us. "The most expensive Martin vintage guitars are from the pre-war period, because by that point they're modern acoustic guitars. The 14-fret steel-string guitars are the most valuable models because they're functional and popular in music today. If you show up on stage with a Stauffer Martin, it's not quite the same!" G

*Guitarist* would like to thank CF Martin & Co

7. This style 45 transition model was acquired by Martin from actor Richard Gere. Recorded as a 00-42S it was shipped to the Bartlett Music Company in LA for $100 on Christmas Day of 1901

*Acoustic*Evolution

# Martin D-18

A true workhorse of the Martin line, this iconic guitar is a zenith of flat-top design

The instrument you see here – Mark Knopfler's 1935 Martin D-18 – represents an apex of acoustic guitar building. Despite the vast technological advances of the post-war period, many would argue this perennially popular design has never been bettered. One of the most imitated flat-top blueprints in history, Martin's Dreadnought (originally spelled Dreadnaught) is the archetypal American acoustic guitar. But it would be a mistake to think that it suddenly appeared from out of nowhere; there was an entire century's worth of innovation leading up to its arrival.

If you look at a Martin headstock from the past 90 years, you'll probably see a decal that reads 'CF Martin & Co Est. 1833'. It was 1932 when the firm began using this transfer – nigh on 100 years after company founder Christian Frederick Martin Sr arrived in New York City in November 1833. Having spent two months on an epic voyage from Germany, the Johann Stauffer-trained luthier set up shop and was producing guitars within months.

During the 1830s, he started moving away from building maple-bodied, figure-of-eight guitars with ornate/moustache bridges and Strat-like Stauffer headstocks in favour of Spanish-style rosewood instruments with smaller upper bouts and rectangular bridges and headstocks. At the same time, he began experimenting with X-bracing and in 1843 produced the first ever X-braced Martin for famed Spanish guitarist Madame de Goñi. 180 years later, this style of bracing is still in use.

Madame de Goñi's X-braced guitar provided noticeable improvements with respect to tone and volume, and dealers soon began asking for "the de Goñi model". Hers was a size 1 guitar. It was the largest Martin available at the time, measuring 12 ¾ inches in width. Seeking to further increase volume and low-end by way of expanding body size, Martin then introduced the 13 ½-inch wide 0 size, followed by the 14 1/8-inch wide 00 size in 1854 and 1858, respectively. It was also during the 1850s that the first style 18 guitars appeared. These instruments were originally constructed using rosewood and cost $18 wholesale (hence the name/designation).

The next important steps in acoustic guitar evolution leading up to the Dreadnought came in 1902. Not only did Martin's first 15-inch wide 000 size guitar,

## CF Martin Sr began experimenting with X-bracing in the 1830s and this style of bracing is still in use today

a 000-21, arrive that year, but so too did the company's first steel-string model, a special order 00-21. While Hawaiian music grew in popularity, Martin began offering steel-string guitars as a regular option in the 1910s. Its first steel-string only model, the 2-17, appeared in 1922 and by the late 1920s, steel strings, rather than gut strings, were the norm.

During this transitional period, Martin built its first ever Dreadnought for Hawaiian musician Mekia Kealakai in 1916. Although the firm began producing Dreadnoughts exclusively for retailers Ditson that year, Martin started branding the large 15 5/8-inch wide D models under its own name in 1931 after the Ditson company folded. Finally, in 1934, Martin changed the Dreadnought from a 12- to 14-fret neck design, following the introduction of its first 14-fret flat-top, the OM-28, in 1929. Now, with its century-long evolution complete, the Martin Dreadnought had at last achieved its iconic form.

This headstock decal first appeared in 1932, almost a century after the company's inception

## The Evolution of the Martin D-18

### 1850s
First 18 Series instruments; rosewood back & sides; spruce top

### 1916
Mekia Kealakai custom Dreadnought; first production Dreadnoughts (Ditson 111 model)

### 1917
18 Series changes from rosewood to mahogany back & sides

### 1923
Steel strings standard for 18 Series

### 1931
First Martin-branded Dreadnoughts (D-1/D-18 and D-2/D-28); 12-fret necks

### 1934
Change from 12- to 14-fret necks

### 1946
Change from ebony to rosewood fretboard & bridge; Sitka spruce replaces Adirondack spruce

### 1969
East Indian rosewood replaces Brazilian rosewood

### Mid-80s
Adjustable truss rod

### 2012
Return to ebony fretboard & bridge

## 1935 Martin D-18

### 1. SERIAL NUMBER
Five-digit number between 58680 and 61947 stamped on neck block

### 2. HEADSTOCK
Decal reads 'C F Martin & Co Est. 1833'; Brazilian rosewood veneer

### 3. PLASTICS
Tortoiseshell celluloid pickguard

### 4. HARDWARE
Ebony belly bridge with six pins; open-back Grover tuners

### 5. BODY
15 5/8 inches wide; Adirondack spruce top; scalloped X-bracing; mahogany back and sides; multiple-ply (b/w) top binding; bound back (b); multiple-ply (b/w) soundhole rings; nitrocellulose lacquer finish

### 6. NECK
Mahogany; steel 'T'-bar reinforced; 25.4-inch scale length; 14th-fret body join; ebony fingerboard; dot inlays to 15th fret; 20 'T' frets; Brazilian rosewood neck heel cap; nitrocellulose lacquer finish

*Acoustic*Evolution

# Martin 0-18

The Martin 0-18 remains small in stature but big on tone…

Martin flat-top acoustic guitars are among some of the most highly regarded instruments of their type. Ever since Christian Friedrich Martin set up shop in the 1830s (originally in New York before moving to their current residence of Nazareth, Pennsylvania a few years later) they have spearheaded acoustic instrument design with several revolutionary technical developments along the way.

Martin's model naming system can sometimes cause a bit of confusion, although once armed with a handful of basic facts it soon becomes clear that a certain logic is at play. It comprises letters and/or numbers separated by a hyphen; the first part describes body shape while the second part describes style in terms of tonewood and ornamentation (generally the higher the number, the fancier the guitar). As far as vintage guitars are concerned, this system has remained consistent since the 1850s and provides a reasonable idea of the spec.

Some of Martin's most popular guitar shapes are (in diminishing size): D or 'dreadnought', 000 or 'auditorium' size, 00 or 'grand concert' size and 0 or 'concert' size. The more numerous styles tend to be (in diminishing levels of fanciness): 45, 35, 28, 18, 17 and 15 – thus, the Martin 0-18 may be thought of in general terms as a smaller-bodied, mid-level instrument. With a body width of 13½ inches and a scale length of 24.9 inches it is larger than the 'parlour' guitars (in fact the term 'parlour guitar' is often defined as any guitar with a body smaller than a Martin 'concert' or 0-size), although it's noticeably much smaller than today's most popular acoustic guitar shape, the dreadnought.

The Martin 0-18 was originally released in 1898 with Brazilian rosewood back and sides, an Adirondack spruce top and an unbound ebony fingerboard. In 1917 the back and sides were changed to mahogany and from 1935 rosewood began to replace ebony as a fingerboard material, becoming standard by 1940. Post-war 18-style guitars

## The 0-18 may be thought of as a mid-level instrument, much smaller than the popular dreadnought shape

have changed little since in terms of body tonewood type, but Martin is currently offering a brand-new model sporting an ebony fretboard with a list price of $2,799 as part of its Standard Series of guitars.

One of the more significant changes to the 0-18's spec came in 1932 when the neck-body join changed from the 12th to the 14th fret, which no doubt took away some of its bottom-end punch, although the guitar is well noted as having a decent attack along with a sweet presence in the upper-mid range, which makes it particularly useful as a recording guitar. Although these smaller-bodied steel string instruments are more often associated with fingerpicking styles like traditional blues, the relatively long scale length of the 0-18 makes it a very respectable strummer (and its diminutive size means it's very good for relaxing and writing on the sofa with!)

A variety of notable guitarists are known to the favour the 0-18 including Steve Earle and Bob Dylan, along with John Frusciante and Warpaint's Emily Kokal in later years.

Steve Howe's 00-18: outwardly similar to the 0-18, but with a slightly larger body size, hence the '00' designation

## The Evolution of the Martin 0-18

**1898**
Introduced with rosewood back and sides; unbound ebony fretboard; rectangular bridge

**1902**
Dot fingerboard markers introduced

**1917**
Mahogany replaces Brazilian rosewood back and sides

**1923**
Steel string bracing

**1932**
Neck-body join changes from 12th to 14th fret

**1935**
Brazilian rosewood fretboards begin to replace ebony fretboards

**1944**
Non-scalloped X-bracing

**1946**
Sitka spruce replaces Adirondack spruce

**1969**
Brazilian rosewood replaced by Indian rosewood

**1996**
Temporarily discontinued

## 1957 Martin 0-18

**1. SERIAL NUMBER**
Six digits stamped into neck block in the 152776 – 159061 range underneath model name "0-18"

**2. HEADSTOCK**
"C F Martin & Co" logo and "EST. 1833" gold silkscreens with black border; Brazilian rosewood veneer

**3. PLASTICS**
Tortoiseshell celluloid pickguard; five-ply alternating black/white top binding with tortoiseshell celluloid outer layer; tortoiseshell celluloid back binding and bottom stripe

**4. HARDWARE**
Open-back Grover Sta-tite tuners; Brazilian rosewood belly bridge with long, rectangular saddle slot

**5. BODY**
4¼ inches deep; Sitka spruce top measuring 13½ inches wide and 18 3/8 inches long; mahogany back and sides; X-bracing; soundhole inlay of nine alternating black/white rings surrounded by two black rings

**6. NECK**
Pronounced v-profile; 24.9-inch scale length glued in mahogany neck with 14th fret body join; 20-fret Brazilian rosewood fingerboard with dot inlays up to 15th fret; Brazilian rosewood heel cap

## DAZED & CONFUSED

# GIBSON 'DREADNOUGHT' JUMBOS

### We decipher some of the mumbo jumbo surrounding Gibson's most popular dreadnoughts…

Gibson's dreadnought designs have been a mainstay of the flat-top world ever since its debut, the Jumbo, was released in 1934. The concept was developed in 1916 when Martin made the 'Extra Grand'-sized 111 and 222 models for music retailers Ditson, while the Dreadnought name was introduced to the Martin line in 1931 with the mahogany D-1 and rosewood D-2 (later renamed the D-18 and D-28).

Taking inspiration from the name of a battleship, Martin applied the Dreadnought/'D' designation to its 15 $5/8$-inch wide, square-shouldered 12-fret-neck flat-tops, and when 14-fret necks became standard in 1934 the Dreadnought design finally settled into what many consider to be the archetypal all-American acoustic guitar. Indeed, the Dreadnought's popularity was so widespread that the brand name eventually became a generic reference for similar-shaped flat-tops made by other builders, including Gibson.

With the release of the 16-inch wide, round-shouldered Jumbo, Gibson set a template for its own Dreadnought, going head to head with Martin in the flat-top market – an increasingly popular area dominated by the Nazareth firm since decades prior. "This greater body size produces a heavy, booming tone so popular today with many players," reads Gibson's 1934 catalogue – a sentiment that still rings true with players almost nine decades later. **G**

## 1 SOUTHERNER JUMBO/ COUNTRY WESTERN

The original $60 Jumbo released in 1934 remained in production until 1936 when it was superseded by the similarly mahogany-bodied $35 Jumbo 35/J-35 and the more upmarket longer-scale, rosewood-bodied Advanced Jumbo. In 1939, the Advanced Jumbo was discontinued and the ornate Jumbo 55/J-55 was added to the line, while a natural finish became optional for the J-35 (sunburst finishes were standard for all of the above models).

During 1942, the Southerner Jumbo replaced the J-55 as Gibson's leading dreadnought and the first models were shipped in August the following year. Immediately recognisable by its L-7 archtop-style large double-parallelogram rosewood-fretboard inlays and sunburst finish, the Southerner Jumbo is also referred to as the Southern Jumbo, or simply the SJ. Its natural finish counterpart appeared in the mid-50s and is variously known as the Country Western and/or SJN (N stands for 'Natural' finish). Both models were discontinued by 1978.

## 2 J-45/J-50

At the beginning of 1942, Gibson's large-bodied flat-top Jumbo line-up consisted of the J-35 and J-55 dreadnoughts, along with the top-of-the-line Super Jumbo/SJ 100 and 200 models. Not to be confused with the SJ-designated Southerner Jumbo, these larger, rounder-bodied flat-tops are alternatively prefixed with a J only and are collectively dubbed 'jumbos' for short (although, strictly speaking, the so-called Gibson 'dreadnoughts' prefixed with a 'J' are also Jumbos).

While the Southerner Jumbo took the spot of the J-55 in 1942, the J-35 was supplanted by the similarly plain, dot-inlayed sunburst J-45 and its natural-finish equivalent, the J-50. A Gibson memo dated August 1942 lists the 'Southern' (Southerner Jumbo) specs with a rosewood back and rim, although this soon changed to mahogany as per the J-45 and J-50. The most significant change to these staple mahogany dreadnoughts occurred when the SJ/N and J-45/50 changed to a square-shouldered design in 1962 and 1969 respectively.

## 3 DOVE

After Gibson/CMI acquired Epiphone in 1957, the company drew up a list of guitars earmarked for production, including some acoustic flat-tops. One of these, described as, "Flattop Jumbo – Maple Back and Rim… Copy Martin D'naught size", was soon to be known as the Epiphone FT-110 Frontier. Released in 1958, this Martin-style/square-shouldered, maple-bodied, 25½-inch-scale length dreadnought was a first for Kalamazoo and laid the foundations for the release of its Gibson equivalent, the Dove, in 1962. As per the Frontier, the Dove measures 16¼ inches in width and came in either sunburst or natural finishes. Aside from its double-parallelogram fretboard inlays, perhaps the most striking features of the Gibson Dove are its elaborately designed, dove-themed, three-pointed pickguard and its dove wing-shaped/inlaid bridge (fitted with a Tune-o-matic until the late 60s). Many have described the Dove's characteristic tone as bright and percussive on account of its maple construction and longer scale length.

## 4 HUMMINGBIRD

You don't need to be an ornithologist to know the difference between a Dove and a Hummingbird but it's more than just bird-themed pickguards that separates these two classic Gibson dreadnoughts. For one, the Hummingbird – Gibson's first square-shouldered dreadnought developed in 1960 – has a shorter 24¾-inch scale length, or at least it did until 1965 when it changed to 25½ inches. And, aside from some rare maple examples produced in the early 60s (known colloquially as 'Humming-Doves'), Hummingbirds are constructed with a mahogany back and rim as standard.

Well regarded as a songwriter's dreadnought, a Gibson brochure titled *New '61 Gibson Guitars & Amplifiers* introduces the Hummingbird as "Gibson's Sensational New Flat Top Guitar… For those interested in owning one of the finest guitars ever made for voice accompaniment." Indeed, from Keith Richards to Thom Yorke, this perennially popular folk-boomer has been used across a huge range of musical styles over the decades since its release.

1

2

3

4

PHOTO BY GIBSON

PHOTO BY GIBSON

*Acoustic*Evolution

# Gibson J-45

Gibson's enduring dreadnought has boomed across the decades

The Gibson J-45 ($45 jumbo) flat-top appeared in 1942 and supplanted the similarly round-shouldered 16-inch-wide Jumbo 35/J-35. Considering the shortages of supplies and labour across the industry during wartime, releasing a new guitar model was a challenging venture for any firm. "In war as in peace," reads a Gibson press ad. "Only a Gibson is good enough… War materials have the right of way at Gibson… We are making some instruments, and some strings, but in limited quantities."

Evidently, Gibson was making provisions for the hard times ahead, and yet despite such austerity the company managed to produce an acoustic model that was not only a success at the time but has since become recognised as one of its most iconic designs. The J-45 – Gibson's "workhorse" acoustic – may not be the fanciest as far as flat-tops go, but it has endured over the decades as an instrument of choice for many, including such notable guitarists as Lightnin' Hopkins, Buddy Holly, David Gilmour and Elliott Smith.

With its spruce top and mahogany back and sides, a typical J-45 may be thought of as the Gibson equivalent to Martin's classic square-shouldered D-18 Dreadnought model, which appeared from 1931 onwards, via the short-lived D-1 (a guitar that was, in turn, developed from the original round-shouldered Martin/Ditson 111 Dreadnought design of 1916). The shortages of materials during the war, however, meant that some J-45s – invariably sporting the wartime 'Only A Gibson Is Good Enough' banner headstock decal – were constructed with maple backs and sides, while others received mahogany tops. All had a Sunburst finish as standard.

The earliest examples feature a very full, rounded neck profile (often referred to as 'baseball bat' necks), which may present an issue for some in terms of playability. For others, the extra mass appears to improve tone with respect to increased volume and sustain. The first J-45s are also notable for their 'firestripe' celluloid teardrop pickguards, but by 1943 the more commonly recognised tortoiseshell celluloid type was standard. In 1955, the pickguard markedly changed shape from a teardrop appearance to a more elongated profile extending

## Despite austerity, Gibson produced an acoustic that is now recognised as one of its most iconic designs

along the treble side of the fretboard and featuring a point facing outwards towards the upper treble bout. Around the same time, an additional (20th) fret was added to the J-45's no-frills rosewood/mother-of-pearl dot inlay fingerboard.

By the following year, a height-adjustable saddle was made optional and would become standard by the early 60s – a mod con that still faces much criticism among aficionados, despite a large amount of popular music having been made and enjoyed using guitars of this type. But perhaps the most questionable of design alterations during the 60s was the introduction of a plastic bridge. These are most commonly seen on J-45s from 1963 to early 1964, before Gibson returned to using a rosewood 'upper belly' bridge. Guitars of the post-40s/50s era can generally be distinguished by a Cherry Sunburst finish introduced in the early part of the 60s.

In 1969, the J-45 received its most radical design alternation: a square-shouldered body profile and the scale was lengthened from 24¾ to 25½ inches. It remained relatively popular in this form in the 70s, but sales steadily declined until it was eventually discontinued in '82, before being reintroduced in '84 in its former guise, resplendent with round shoulders, a teardrop pickguard and a 24¾-inch scale length. G

## The Evolution of the Gibson J-45

**1942**
J-45 introduced; round shoulders; 24¾-inch scale; firestripe teardrop pickguard

**1943**
Tortoiseshell celluloid teardrop pickguard

**1946**
"Only A Gibson Is Good Enough" headstock banner discontinued

**1947**
Modernised script Gibson headstock logo replaces longhand script type

**1949**
Upper belly bridge standard

**1955**
Longer pickguard (extends along fretboard) with point facing upper treble bout

**1956**
Height-adjustable saddle available (standard by 1960)

**1969**
Lower belly bridge standard; square shoulders; 25½" scale

**1970**
Double X-bracing

**1982**
Discontinued

## 1947 Gibson J-45

**1. SERIAL NUMBER**
Factory order number (FON) comprises four-digit batch number followed by two-digit instrument rank number ink stamped on inside/back; 'J45' ink stamped on back brace

**2. HEADSTOCK**
'Made In USA' impressed into upper rear; gold silk-screened modernised Gibson logo; black nitrocellulose finish

**3. HARDWARE**
Three-on-a-plate single-line Kluson Deluxe tuners; Brazilian rosewood upper belly bridge with fixed saddle

**4. NECK**
Single-piece mahogany glued-in neck; unbound 19-fret Brazilian rosewood fingerboard with mother-of-pearl dot markers

**5. BODY**
16 inches wide; round shoulders; flat spruce top with Sunburst finish and three-ply (w/b/w) binding; w/b/w soundhole rings; single-bound mahogany back; mahogany sides

**6. PLASTICS**
Black bridge pins; white tuner buttons; tortoiseshell celluloid teardrop pickguard; black 'bell' truss rod cover

*Guitarist* would like to thank Vintage 'n' Rare Guitars

*Acoustic*Evolution

# Gibson SJ-200

### Gibson's supersize acoustic has always been the "king of flat-tops"

Gibson's SJ-200 acoustic guitar first appeared in the 1930s. Around this time, Gibson and Epiphone were going head to head in a size war – each trying to outdo the other under the premise 'bigger is better' while equating instrument dimensions with power, projection and, ultimately, status. This spirit of competition led to several developments, notably Gibson's 18-inch-wide Super 400 and Epiphone's 18½-inch-wide Emperor. These supersize archtops were deemed flagship models, and both sat at the top of their respective price lists with a $400 tag. Along with the Super 400, Gibson unveiled its Jumbo flat-top (named after the colossal elephant) in 1934 in order to compete directly with Martin's large-body Dreadnought design (named after the gigantic battleship). Also in '34, Gibson's seminal L-5 archtop (which celebrates its 100th anniversary this year) was "Advanced" from 16 to 17 inches in width.

It was only a matter of time before Gibson introduced a supersize flat-top with the kind of ornamentation that set its leading archtops apart, and the SJ-200 took many of its cues from the Advanced L-5. In fact, from its 1937 debut, early examples of the SJ-200 were labelled "L-5 Spec". As well as having a similar body shape and size, the SJ-200 sports an L-5-style bound, pointed fingerboard. Along with fancy inlays and multiple-ply body binding the similarities are clear. The most famous of these early custom-order prototype guitars belonged to 'singing cowboy' Ray Whitley. The bygone era of singing cowboys was a Hollywood phenomenon, and Gibson jumped at the chance to supply a rapidly growing demand among the celebrities of the day. Gene Autry, Ray 'Crash' Corrigan, Jimmy Wakely and other cowboy movie stars all appeared with Gibson's "king of the flat-tops". And with silver screen endorsements of such calibre, the instrument soon gained iconic status.

First appearing in Gibson's 1938 catalogue, the $200 "Super Jumbo" was renamed the Super Jumbo 200 (hence SJ-200) by the following year. After the war, it was advertised simply as the J-200 but continued to be labelled "SJ-200" well into the 1950s. Consequently, either name is used to refer to the same model. And though the rounder-bodied S/J-200, J-180 and J-185 guitars are often dubbed Jumbos exclusively, many Dreadnought-style Gibson flat-top models are also, strictly speaking, Jumbos (J-45, J-50, J-55

## Gibson introduced a supersize flat-top in the 30s with ornamentation that set its leading archtops apart

et cetera). Additionally, it's worth noting the 'S' designation should not be confused with the Gibson SJ/Southerner Jumbo/Southern Jumbo.

The singing cowboys may have helped popularise the SJ-200 in the beginning, but the model is perhaps better known as an instrument of choice for the likes of the Everly Brothers, Elvis Presley, Tom Petty, Orianthi, Bob Dylan and Pete Townshend – all of whom have been honoured by Gibson with signature models. Emmylou Harris, too, is an SJ-200 devotee. The Grammy-winning acoustic legend even custom-ordered a guitar from Gibson based on her ex-Gram Parsons SJ-200. She also collaborated on a unique signature model – the L-200 – that features a reduced width of 15 inches. Similarly, players who think the SJ-200's 17-inch width is a bit too much might find the smaller J-180/Everly Brothers and J-185 guitars more comfortable to play.

*Truly a top-of-the-line instrument, it's hard to find a better example of bookmatched high-grade maple than this*

## The Evolution of the Gibson SJ-200

### 1937
L-5-style custom-order instrument presented to Ray Whitley

### 1938
Advertised in catalogue as "Super Jumbo" priced $200; sunburst finish; rosewood back/sides

### 1939
Renamed Super Jumbo 200; mahogany Super Jumbo 100 released ($100)

### 1941
Ebony fingerboard changes to rosewood

### 1942
Double X-bracing changes to single X-bracing

### 1947
Advertised as J-200; maple back/sides

### 1948
Natural finish available (J-200N)

### 1961
'Closed'/Tune-o-matic bridge replaces 'open' bridge with non-adjustable saddle

### 1970s
Dove-style bridge with non-adjustable saddle; double X-bracing

### Current
Several SJ-200 models in Original, Modern, Artist and Custom

*Acoustic*Evolution

### 1953 Gibson J-200N

**1. SERIAL NUMBER**
'A'-prefixed five-digit serial number inked on oval orange soundhole label

**2. HEADSTOCK**
Bound; mother-of-pearl Gibson logo and 'crown' motif; black nitrocellulose finish (face and rear) with 'bee sting' taper

**3. HARDWARE**
Gold-plated Kluson Deluxe tuners; rosewood 'moustache' bridge with four pearl ribbon inlays; non-adjustable saddle

**4. NECK**
25½-inch scale length; laminated figured maple; bound 20-fret pointed rosewood fingerboard with mother-of-pearl 'crest'/'cloud'/'pineapple' inlays

**5. BODY**
17 inches wide; spruce top with seven-ply (b/w) binding; figured maple rim; two-piece figured maple back with five-ply (b/w) binding and 'zipper' centre stripe; seven- and three-ply (b/w) soundhole rings; Natural finish

**6. PLASTICS**
White bridge pins; white keystone tuner buttons; engraved celluloid pickguard; black/white 'bell' truss rod cover; three-ply (b/w) heel cap

PHOTO BY JOLLY CURTIS

*Acoustic*Evolution

# Gibson LG Series

Introduced during the war, these small flat-tops were a mix and match of greatness

From the early 1940s, guitar-building materials were in increasingly short supply due to America's war effort. Furthermore, following President Roosevelt's formation of the War Production Board, Gibson was forced to turn its attention to the manufacture of military hardware. These monumental changes may have signalled the end of the Kalamazoo firm had it not been for the immense efforts of the female staff who, against the odds, not only helped keep guitar production going but also happened to create some of the finest flat-tops to ever leave the factory. Crafted between 1942 and 1946, these revered wartime instruments are often referred to as 'Banner' guitars on account of a headstock decal that reads 'Only a Gibson is good enough'.

Appearing in 1942, the 14¼-inch-wide LG series fleshed out a limited range of wartime flat-tops, which also included the L-00, J-45 and Southerner Jumbo. Many will already be familiar with the LG series model names (LG-0, LG-1, LG-2, LG-2¾ and LG-3), although their appearances, disappearances, reappearances and redesignations has caused much confusion. Muddying the waters even further is the fact that specifications chopped and changed from one guitar to the next in the early days due to material shortages.

The sunburst LG-2 and its natural-finish equivalent, the LG-3, were both introduced in 1942. As was the sunburst J-45 along with its natural-finish counterpart, the J-50. However, because of the difficulty in obtaining "good enough" quality tonewood for the plain tops, both the LG-3 and J-50 were temporarily discontinued until after the war (a total of 130 and 144 of each were shipped between '42 to '43 respectively). As the sunburst models were able to disguise imperfections in tonewood more easily, Gibson soon began using the finish exclusively.

The first LG-1 was shipped in 1943, as was the first Southerner Jumbo. The original incarnation of the LG-1 features X-bracing as per the LG-2 and LG-3. However, unlike its spruce-topped siblings, the Banner LG-1 features a mahogany soundboard; a stain finish further sets it apart. A mere 139 of these rare LG-1s left the factory – 138

## The LG-0 was released for "students, strolling players, and anyone who wants to have fun with the guitar"

in '43 and the final one in '44. When the LG-1 reappeared after the war it did so with a sunburst spruce top. Thus it appears similar to the LG-2, although its budget-end lateral/'ladder' bracing provides a more midrange-focused sound.

In 1958, the LG-0 was released as a budget guitar for "students, teachers, strolling players, and anyone who wants to have fun with the guitar". Like the post-war LG-1, the LG-0 is ladder-braced. It featured an all-mahogany construction until '68 when a spruce top was fitted as standard (at the same time, the LG-1 was discontinued). While the LG-0 model was aimed at the lower end of the market, it is considered by many players to be a very respectable guitar indeed.

Similarly, the ladder-braced LG-2¾ appeared in 1949 marketed as "ideal for children or players with small hands". Regardless, this unique Gibson has found favour with many a pro player. Guitarist Martin Barre of Jethro Tull fame and singer-songwriter Arlo Guthrie – son of the great Woody Guthrie – both used LG-2¾ Gibsons, while Fender and Rickenbacker author Martin Kelly is never too far away from his favourite "kitchen guitar".

*The respectable LG-2¾ was marketed as "ideal for children or players with small hands"*

## The Evolution of the Gibson LG Series

**August 1942**
First LG-2 shipped; first LG-3 shipped; mahogany backs/sides; spruce tops

**April 1943**
First LG-1 shipped; all-mahogany

**1943**
LG-3 and LG-1 production suspended; some LG-2s with maple backs/mahogany tops

**1944**
Switch from Adirondack to Sitka spruce tops

**1946**
Headstock banner discontinued; LG-1 and LG-3 production recommences

**1949**
LG-2¾ released

**1958**
LG-0 released; all-mahogany; discontinued 1973

**1962**
LG-2, LG-2¾ and LG-3 superseded by B-25, B-25¾ and B-25N respectively

**1968**
B-25¾ and LG-1 discontinued; LG-0 now with spruce top

**1977**
Last B-25 and B-25N models shipped

**Martin Barre's 1950s Gibson LG-2¾**

**1. SERIAL NUMBER**
Factory order number (FON) ink stamped inside; number prefixed by letter (denoting year)

**2. HEADSTOCK**
Gold silk-screened Gibson logo; black nitrocellulose face

**3. HARDWARE**
Kluson tuners with white keystone buttons (replacements); rectangular Brazilian rosewood bridge with fixed saddle

**4. NECK**
Glued-in; single-piece mahogany; shorter 22¾-inch scale length; unbound 19-fret Brazilian rosewood fingerboard with mother-of-pearl dot markers

**5. BODY**
12 11/16 inches wide; ladder-braced Sitka spruce top with sunburst finish and three-ply (w/b/w) binding; w/b/w soundhole rings; single-bound mahogany back; mahogany sides

**6. PLASTICS**
White bridge pins; tortoiseshell celluloid pickguard; black 'bell' truss-rod cover

Acoustic Evolution

# Epiphone F.T. 110/Frontier

When Epiphone went to Kalamazoo, a new Frontier beckoned…

Debuting in Epiphone's 1942 catalogue priced at $110, the 15 7/8-inch-wide 'Jumbo Size' F.T. 110 supplanted the similarly maple-bodied top-of-the-line F.T. De Luxe (flat-top version of De Luxe archtop model) released earlier in 1939. Hailed as 'Truly the Artist's Choice!', the F.T. 110 featured a single-bound 20-fret rosewood fingerboard with distinctive slotted-block mother-of-pearl inlays. In 1949, its square-shouldered profile morphed into a rounder design with a 'tone back' laminated back and it remained in production throughout the company's slow decline into the mid-50s.

Following the death of company founder, Epaminondas 'Epi' Stathopoulo, in 1943, Epiphone found itself increasingly plagued with internal quarrels, labour issues and supply problems with materials, resulting in Epi's surviving brother and company president, Orphie, telephoning Gibson president Ted McCarty to propose a buyout. On 10 May 1957, Epiphone's acquisition (for the sum of $20,000!) was announced by Ted, and in early 1958, he suggested a list of several Epiphone-branded guitar models that could be built at Gibson's Kalamazoo factory. This included a 'Flattop Jumbo – Maple Back and Rim… Copy Martin D'naught size, Epiphone head veneer, pickguard and fingerboard…' and it was soon decided the F.T. 110's production was to continue, albeit under a new model name: the FT-110 Frontier.

With square shoulders and a solid construction – including a five-ply bound maple back, maple sides and a seven-ply bound spruce top – the Frontier's body measures 16 1/4 inches in width and was finished in either Sunburst or Natural. While utilising Epiphone parts from the previous period of production, existing F.T. 110 V-profile laminated necks (identifiable by an 'E' script headstock logo) were used up until 1962 when the Kalamazoo-made one-piece mahogany necks (identifiable by a 'slashed-C' script headstock logo) became standard. Both the older 'New York' and the newer Kalamazoo necks have a scale length of 25 1/2 inches and feature a single-bound 20-fret rosewood fingerboard with slotted-block mother-of-pearl inlays.

Also in 1962, the Frontier received an adjustable saddle as standard in place of the existing fixed type, and the original teardrop pickguard was replaced by a larger, fancier design depicting a Western-themed scene featuring lassos and cacti. In 1963, the headstock was lengthened in tandem with the arrival of a black-and-white laminated plastic truss rod cover sporting a 'slashed-C' epsilon logo, making the transitory permutation of 'short headstock with lassos and cacti pickguard' a rare and desirable spec combination.

## By 1966, the Frontier's wide nut width had narrowed giving the guitar a distinctly different feel

By 1965, the Frontier's original wide nut width had decreased from 1 11/16 inches to 1 5/8 inches, and by 1966, it had narrowed to 1 9/16 inches, giving the guitar a distinctly different feel. Around that time, the earlier-style teardrop pickguard began to reappear sporadically alongside the 'lassos and cacti' scratchplate, until the latter was eventually phased out in the late 60s.

While building Epiphone-branded guitars proved successful (peaking at around 20 per cent of Kalamazoo's total output of instruments during 1965), by the end of the decade, both Gibson and Epiphone production had declined to a mere fraction of its mid-60s zenith. Gibson's 'golden era' president, Ted McCarty, had parted ways in 1966, build quality had been increasingly compromised under the weight of demand, and following the acquisition of company owners CMI in 1969 by ECL (renamed Norlin in 1970), FT-110 Frontier production ceased at the turn of the 70s.

*One-piece mahogany necks with a short/non-elongated headstock were made during 1962 and 1963*

## The Evolution of the Epiphone FT-110N Frontier

**1939**
16 1/2" wide F.T. De Luxe top of F.T. (flat-top) range; maple back & sides

**1942**
'Jumbo Size' F.T. 110 top of F.T. range; square shoulders; maple back & sides

**1949**
Rounded shoulders; 'tone back' laminated maple arched back

**1954**
Width increases from 15 7/8" to 16"

**1958**
Kalamazoo -110/N Frontiers; 16 1/4" wide; square shoulders; laminated neck; fixed saddle

**1962**
One-piece mahogany neck; adjustable saddle; 'lassos and cacti' large celluloid pickguard

**1963**
Elongated headstocks with epsilon logo truss rod cover

**1965**
1 11/16" nut width decreases to 1 5/8"

**1966**
1 9/16" nut width now standard

**1970**
Discontinued following Gibson/CMI 1969 ECL/Norlin acquisition

128 | LEGENDARY GUITARS

### 1963 Epiphone FT-110N Frontier

**1. SERIAL NUMBER**
Six digits ink-stamped onto blue rectangular soundhole label corresponding with six digits impressed into rear of headstock (label also reads 'Style FT-100N' and 'Epiphone Frontier')

**2. HEADSTOCK**
Short/non-elongated profile; black painted holly veneer with nitrocellulose clearcoat; 'slashed-C' script logo mother-of-pearl inlay; oval design mother-of-pearl inlay

**3. PLASTICS**
Transparent celluloid pickguard with lassos-and-cacti design; black/white laminated pointed/arched truss rod cover; six white bridge pins

**4. HARDWARE**
Gold-plated single-line Kluson Deluxe tuners with plastic keystone buttons; rosewood bridge with white ceramic adjustable saddle

**5. BODY**
Square shoulders; 16¼ inches wide; 4⅞ inches deep; Sitka spruce top with seven-ply alternating (black/white) binding; soundhole inlays of seven alternating (black/white) rings surrounded by three (white/black/white) rings; curly maple back with five-ply alternating (black/white) binding; curly maple sides; Natural finish (hence 'N' in model name)

**6. NECK**
25½-inch scale length; one-piece mahogany with 14th fret body join; single-bound 20-fret rosewood fingerboard with slotted-block mother-of-pearl inlays; Natural finish

*By 1962, the fixed bridge saddle had been replaced with an adjustable design of white ceramic or wood*

*A Kalamazoo-style rectangular blue-paper soundhole label*

# Subscribe here

## SUBSCRIBE TO GUITARIST, TOTAL GUITAR OR GUITAR TECHNIQUES & SAVE 45%*

**+ NEW DIGITAL ACCESS**

**SAVE 45%**

**SUBSCRIBE ONLINE AT: www.magazinesdirect.com/D47S**

**OR CALL: 0330 333 1113 AND QUOTE CODE D47S**

Lines are open Mon-Fri 8.30am-7pm & Sat 10am-3pm (UK Time)

**OFFER ENDS: 28 JUNE 2025**

**Terms & Conditions** Offer closes 28 June 2025. Price is guaranteed for the first 6 months, please allow up to 6 weeks for the delivery of your first subscription issue (up to 8 weeks overseas) the subscription rate includes postage and packaging. *Savings are based on the cover price. Payment is non-refundable after the 14-day cancellation period. **Access to the digital library will end with your subscription. For full terms and conditions, visit www.magazinesdirect.com/terms. For enquiries and overseas rates please call: +44 (0) 330 333 1113. Lines are open Monday-Friday 8:30am-7pm, Saturday 10am-3pm UK Time (excluding Bank Holidays) or email: help@magazinesdirect.com. Calls to 0330 numbers will be charged at no more than a national landline call, and may be included in your phone provider's call bundle.